REBUILDING THE BROKEN WALL

Being Empowered To Take Responsibility
For Your Success

Tobi Adegboyega

All scripture quotations, unless otherwise indicated, are taken from the New King James Version®.
Copyright©1982 by Thomas Nelson, Inc. Used by permission. All rights reserved.

REBUILDING THE BROKEN WALL
Copyright © Tobi Adegboyega 2010

ISBN: 978-0-9566745-1-7

Published by TheVine Publishing
Tel: 0208 279 3564
Printed in United Kingdom

All rights reserved. No part of this publication may be reproduced, stored in a retrieval system, or transmitted in any form or by any means, mechanical, electronic, photocopying or otherwise without prior written consent of the copyright owner.

DEDICATION

To men and women who are passionate about the truth; to those who have a genuine compassion for humanity; to the crusaders of truth, justice and freedom - those who are alive and those who have departed. This book is dedicated as a voice for practical freedom.

I have chosen to start from my constituency, the church. I have also chosen to start my crusade, speaking to believers, to wake up and fulfill their destiny.

I believe this would spread to everywhere of human endeavour. I dedicate my life to empowering people and inspiring humanity to true success.

This book is therefore dedicated to humanity.

CONTENTS

DEDICATION	3
ACKNOWLEDGMENTS	7
INTRODUCTION	9
Chapter 1: Knowing The Truth Shall Set You Free	20
Chapter 2: My Journey	26
Chapter 3: The Rebuilding Process	36
Chapter 4: The Laws For Rebuilding	54
Chapter 5: In All Your Getting, Get Understanding	85
Chapter 6: Your Authority As A Believer	117
Chapter 7: Wisdom Is The Principal Thing	129
Chapter 8: The Wise Make Plans	157
Chapter 9: After All Is Said And Done	178
Chapter 10: How Long Will It Take? Not Long!	185
NOTES	

ACKNOWLEDGMENTS

There is only one who gives gifts, talents and ability to men and women in order for them to use these abilities to bring meaning to humanity. I first acknowledge the Creator of humanity as my source and strength.

My parents gave me a good head-start and opportunity to be a minister of the truth, I thank them.

Everyone around me has been a true blessing. I therefore acknowledge and thank all those who are part of this struggle to bring the light into the church, to restore our nation and to free humanity. Thank you all for your support. You have believed in me and have supported this work.

This book is just a very little fragment of a huge work we are about to do in this generation; we are just about to start. I have been to the mountain top and I see a true church arising with a new people and we (the church) would again be the light of the world!

INTRODUCTION

About two years ago, after reading through the book of Nehemiah for almost the 100th time in my life, I had a conviction to re-read through this book of Nehemiah one more time on that same day. I was a bit reluctant at first because I had read it over and over again. I have even made a 'good sermon' out of it, so I thought 'why should I read through it the second time in a single day?' I wanted to read other passages but I was obedient and read through it all the same time.

I have always seen the book of Nehemiah as an interesting historical writing but the only thing that I failed to see until that very day was that it was also life changing. Of course, I believe every passage, story and parable in the bible is life changing, however, I could not see how much life was in Nehemiah's story. It wasn't really Nehemiah's story but rather a story of rebuilding.

It was and still is the story of a man who was willing to make an impact by taking responsibility to reconstruct a nation at its worst state; rebuilding people's lives and destiny even when it seemed like there was no more hope at all. Nehemiah was the man that rebuilt the broken walls of Israel, signifying the restoration of glory.

After reading this passage again, I discovered some vital keys that people must possess in order to restore their nations, family, society and relationship etc. I discovered that there are some things God cannot do until men decide to take responsibility. I discovered that national reformation is in the hands of the people of that nation and without them standing up to restore their nation, the state of the nation will remain the same no matter how much time they spend asking God to come and reform their nation. This also applies to our personal lives.

Until we rise to do some things, nothing positive will happen in our lives. Therefore, the process of rebuilding is solely in our hands, but there are principles to follow. God created the heavens and earth and he set laws into motions so that those who understand and walk by these laws may benefit from it.

It is because of this understanding of laws and principles that you might find some statements in this book 'controversial'. I believe in prayers and all form of religious exercises but I have seen the limitations of these ever increasing religious activities by men and women's involvement in them.

The religious world today teaches us to end all our complaints about the injustices in the world in the four corners of a wall claiming that we are praying about these problem(s). However, a man like Nehemiah would pray and then decide to put some principles to work. This is why this book is an attempt to discourage us from thinking the way we used to think, sharply dismissing some practices, even though they look like they are trendy in the religious world today.

The chapters and statements in this book will either open your eyes or cause you distress. Whichever one, I still want to ask that you read with an open mind and not a religious mind. An open heart will lead to revelation and the revelation will lead to revolution; this will certainly bring a change into your life.

Martin Luther King Junior, like Nehemiah decided to pursue a vision of rebuilding and he did this with his life. People of his time may not have seen him as your typical 'pastor' because he didn't sound or dress like one; but I believe he birthed a change that would become a true legacy for generations to come. I believe this is what God has called us to, not just to build institutions and monuments but to build a true legacy. We cannot do this without first rebuilding our own lives and relationships; getting back to the original plan of God for our lives and destiny.

After reading the book of Nehemiah, as I was instructed to, I saw clearer and immediately knew that this was a message for my generation for this season. However, what is the message and to whom specifically is the message for? Then I heard the topic 'rebuild' or 'rebuilding the broken walls.'

It is important for me to explain what this means. Even though it looks simple and self explanatory, I still believe that it is specific for some set of people and organisations. The first message in the title is the issue of re-building. I will like to break this topic down, defining every word to bring clarity and precision to what I believe would be accomplished in this book.

1. RE-BUILD

The word 'Re' mentioned in the book title is a prefix, occurring originally from the Latin word - meaning 'again' and 'again' to indicate repetition or with the meaning 'back' or backwards to indicate withdrawal or backwards motion; regenerate, refurbish, retype, retrace, revert etc. This all shows us that it is not new work. It is something that has once been done but along the line something went wrong and it is now no longer the way it should be.

The temple of Solomon was built with great dignity and sophistication. When Israel started disobeying God again, their enemies rose against them, destroyed them and plundered the temple of Solomon. This temple had all sorts of gold and expensive art works in it. Everything was taken away. The temple was left totally empty. In the bid to cover the shameful state of the temple that was once the pride of the nations, they (Israel) replaced gold with bronze, just to make the temple not empty until another king came generations after. He discovered what had happened and he decided to restore the temple to its original state, which is this 're-building' - returning it to the way it is supposed to be or designed to be.

INTRODUCTION

There are those of us who know that where we are right now is not where we are really supposed to be. In fact, some years ago, we thought that by now we ought to have been much better off; achieving some great things. However along the line, something went wrong. A mistake or a wrong decision was made and now we have settled where we are because it seems like nothing else can be done.

Nehemiah teaches us that it doesn't matter how wrong things have gone, there is still something called 're' or 'again'. He teaches from his actions that the walls through some principles could be built again. Also, Nehemiah teaches us that all nations can be built again if we have leaders who take responsibilities and have positive visions for the nations and also if the church would have true leaders who are interested in building lives and not empires.

The word 'build' means to construct by assembly and joining parts or materials, to establish, increase of, strengthen, to mould, form or create. So, to rebuild is to reconstruct by assembling and joining parts of materials. Nehemiah built the broken walls of Israel again. He brought it back to the way it used to be and to the way it was supposed to be. You can do the same also, through the principles shared in this book. You can bring your nations, church or life to the way it is supposed to be. No matter what has happened in times past, you can still be everything you've once dreamt of being.

2. KNOW 'THE' BROKEN WALLS IN YOUR LIFE?

The second word in the title (rebuilding the broken walls) is the word 'THE'. This, in the context of this book and the narration of Nehemiah, stands for something specific. There was a specific assignment for Nehemiah to accomplish, which was to rebuild a certain broken wall. You also have a specific wall to rebuild. I strongly believe that every man or woman has a specific wall to rebuild. It could be personal and national like Nehemiah.

If anyone says they have no walls to rebuild, it could be that they are just living in their own world and not looking beyond themselves into the nation and their society. There is always a wall to rebuild but having said that, we must understand that at certain periods of our lives, we have to be specific so that we can maintain focus in order be able to measure success or accomplishment.

Nehemiah took the responsibility upon himself to build the wall and not to lead a war that would set them free from captivity even though that looked important as well. 'Rebuild the' - the specific thing(s) that comes to your mind as you read this word is what you should first attempt to do by the principles in this book. It could be your finances, your relationship with the Lord or important people in your life. It could be your nation. Whatever it is, be specific!

Martin Luther King Jr had a specific wall to rebuild in a specific place (United States of America). Moses had an assignment to bring Israel out of Egypt, but Joshua had the assignment to bring them into the Promised Land.

Know that specific wall you are meant to rebuild right now and always have it at the forefront of your mind. Write it somewhere you can see and as you read further in this book, you will be able to see more clearly 'the' specific areas to rebuild.

3. BROKEN

The word 'Broken' can mean reduced to fragments, fragmented, ruptured, torn, fractured or not functioning properly; out of working, incomplete, weakened in strength and in spirit.

The more we define these words, the more they come to life. I cannot count how many broken lives I have met in counseling, people whose situations looked impossible to amend. After reading the book of Nehemiah, we were able to learn and apply the principles in this book in the end what looked impossible became possible because they changed their way of thinking. They saw things from a better and clearer perspective.

It doesn't matter how broken you are, if in the middle of being broken you can see clearly then you will be rebuilt. There is a chapter in this book titled 'What do you see?' It will explain more about seeing clearly.

If we go back into the definition of 'rebuild' and especially the word 'build', it talks about putting bits and pieces together again. Being broken means to be torn apart or being incomplete; the principles discussed in this book will give you practical 'raw' materials that can help you to put together; to rebuild the broken and torn apart elements in your life or nation. God Almighty is a master builder. He gives us practical steps to take in order to rebuild what has been broken.

4. WALLS

Walls signify protection, covering and glory for Israel. At that time, a walled city meant a glorious and beautiful city. That wall was both their pride and defence. When a person has made lot of mistakes and wrong decisions in life, soon their lives begin to go in the wrong direction and when this begins to happen they become very vulnerable.

They become a prey to their thought and people around them. Their thoughts begin to betray them. They think they are failures and cannot seem to think positively. They think that they are meant to be poor or at most be mediocre.

Their walls are broken and their defence is no longer there. Sometimes, the challenges of life are not even based on having made mistakes or wrong decisions but life just happened like that. Whatsoever it may be, Nehemiah showed us know the broken walls can be rebuilt again.

PUTTING THE PUZZLES TOGETHER

If you now put all these words together, I believe you will get a clear picture of what has been laid on my heart to discuss with you in this book. I totally denounce religion and all that it stands for. Religion has no power or force whatsoever to change a man or his condition. Relationship however has power to change man so that man can change his world by God's word.

I have not attempted to share some religious beliefs in this book, but rather to help us dispel some religious beliefs that has kept us in bondage and rendered us inactive by making us believe that God would come down and change things for us.

I have also tried to make us understand, especially those coming from 'developing' nations who believe that there are certain spiritual powers that can stop us from being successful at building and rebuilding our lives and as a result, we become very religious and fall victim to false teachings and endless religious prayers. However, we can achieve anything that God has placed in our hearts to accomplish in our generation through wisdom, knowledge and through the principles set in the book of Nehemiah.

Apart from studies that I have done to put this book together, my life also is what I have put into words. The things I have seen and what I believe God deliberately allowed me to see in my life and the past generation. I have looked through the eyes of religion, growing up from a church background and have also been taught by the world after choosing to live without God for many years. I have been able to understand why some things work and others have not worked. I will mention some of them in this book.

If it is possible, I want to change what you have been trained to believe so that we can go for what really works. I believe that as you read this book, you will be able to put all sentiment away and allow the spirit to give you a new outlook on your life.

You can rebuild the broken walls.

Chapter 1

KNOWING THE TRUTH SHALL SET YOU FREE

'And you shall know the truth and the truth shall set you free - Jesus Christ (John 8:32)

My heart aches so much when I see people - men, women and the youth who have a lot to offer; people with so much energy, wisdom and talent to change the world but their own world has come crumbling down. Sometimes it makes me cry and I get filled with doubts and questions about those very things I have believed from my childhood.

Speaking of my childhood, I believe it is very important that I share my background with you. First of all, it is highly imperative for anyone reading this book to understand that what I intend to do is to give practical steps to everyone; these are steps that will help us to rebuild our lives and get back to our original destiny - the true purpose for our lives. I understand that for me to do this, the first thing I need to emphasise is the word 'Truth'.

'Truth is the only force that sets one free. True and real deliverance is in *knowing* the 'truth'; the truth about our lives, circumstances, the truth about God and his way of doing things because without the knowledge of truth, man remains under bondage.

'All truths are easy to understand once they are discovered…the point is to discover them - Galileo Galilei

Man thinks he can be free from the struggles of life by spending more time in the world, or if he happens to be religious - he believes he can be free by his involvement in some spiritual exercises. Unfortunately, today's church of Christ which is supposed to be the ground and pillar of the 'truth', is confused about the truth itself.

'I wrote to you so that you know how to conduct yourselves in the house of God, the church of the living God, the ground and pillar of the truth. (1st Timothy 3:15)

I believe the church, according to the scriptures, is a place where all nations should be able to go into so that they can know the mind of God, walk in his ways and therefore be wise. However today, the church goes to the world to learn its ways and brings this way into the church.

We see men preying on the ignorance of another man to build themselves empires; sometimes these men are also deceived by their own greed or lust; and the effect of this on the people is continuous suffering, unending afflictions, broken dreams, shattered lives and a lack of greatness because anything less than the truth will not work for the people. Jesus said *'And you shall know the truth and the truth shall set you free* . (John 8:32)

In this book, I present to you the 'truth' that will help to rebuild your life, dreams and most importantly God's purpose for your life. Coming from my background to where I am now, I believe my journey in life has been 'programmed' by God in order to know these truths and to share them with you without any fear of being labelled 'controversial.' I have refused to change many lines and words in this book and refrained from being 'politically correct' to the detriment of the truth because I believe the 'truth' contained here will help many to build their destiny and get back on track with our manufacturer (God).

Growing up, I departed completely from the Lord. It was like going from one extreme end of loving God and walking with him to the far extreme end of just desiring life and its pleasures. Like many of us '*Pastor s children*, I became a total rebel even though within me, the love for God was still very much in existent; I just couldn't look for him the way I used to.

I got heavily involved in alcohol, drugs and all sorts of vices that I would never have imagined myself getting into some years before. I believe strongly that my own case is not just like any other 'pastor's son' scenario; mine was destiny. When I look today at how many lives and destiny the Lord has made me touch in the nations, I know He allowed me to go through the backsliding route for a purpose.

It is important for me to say that whilst growing up 'doing the right things', praying and studying the Word of God; pride and self righteousness were also developing in me. I thought being righteous was judged by what we do and I was better than the rest of my friends because I did not do what they did. If I had continued at the pace I was going back then, there is no way I would be who I have become today.

It has been much easier for me to help 'prostitutes', 'drunkards' and 'drug addicts' because of the route God took me through. (I am not suggesting that you cannot help such people if you have not been there or done what they are doing. I am just saying that I believe in destiny and we are all wired in different ways.)

My process of growing up has been from one extreme to another until the time God said 'I want to use you; I want you to rebuild the broken walls in your life; I want you to enter into your destiny'. I thank God for my praying parents; as a parent you can help rebuild the life of your children in the place of prayer. Yes, it is good to talk to them and form a strong relationship with them but it is also important to understand that rebuilding starts in the place of prayer.

We will look into this in the chapters to come.

Chapter 2

MY JOURNEY

After many years of running from the Lord, I finally had to stop running and knew it was time to rebuild what had been broken. My heart began to yearn for the Lord again like before, but by then, there were so many things in my life that I had been addicted to over many years. I was confused and troubled. I thought to myself, 'how on earth am I going to get off these addictions?'

I couldn't even pray like I could years before and imagined that God hated me for all the things I'd done; I thought that I couldn't even go back to God until I really got rid of those things. I was trained to believe that way but this thought- process only produced confusion for me until one day I begged God for mercy saying,

CHAPTER TWO

"Lord I would like to do your work again but I can't because I am doing this and that (drugs and alcohol etc) and I am addicted to the wrong things". I also promised God that if He set me free, then I would do His work again.

I suddenly heard in my spirit, '*You go ahead and do my work and you will be free*. I was thinking, 'No way Lord, you wouldn't like that because anyone that will do your work must be sort of *"perfect"* or at least shouldn't be doing what I'm doing'. Unfortunately, this is the image our pastors present to us about God and the way he is but only to eventually find out that it is false. I decided to go ahead; disregarding the way I have been programmed and to carry out God's work - even with my faults.

In doing this, I saw the Power of God break the addictions in my life; I will never forget this experience. If you have never been addicted to anything before, you may not understand how powerful what I am saying is, but if you have been or still are - take the same steps and see the power of God set you free.

God's love never departs from us because of what we do or what we do not do. He (Christ) has done it all for us. We just need to accept what He has done, and allow Him to work in us, and step by step, we are being moulded to become what the Lord wants us to become.

My Growth in the Scriptures

Effective Christianity affects our community, the society and then the nations. There is no way I can write words or give talks without talking about the church because I believe that the Church is the hope of the nations.

"Now it shall come to pass in the latter days that the mountain of the Lord s house shall be established on the top of the mountains and shall be exalted about the hills; and all nations shall flow to it

"Many people shall come and say, come and let us go up to the mountain of the Lord -To the house of the God of Jacob; He will teach us His ways and we shall walk in His paths. For out of Zion shall go forth the law and the Word of the Lord from Jerusalem" - (Isaiah 2:1-5).

A dying church cannot heal dying nations. If a country is sick, observe the churches in that country and ask yourself why there are so many churches springing up and yet the nations do not regard them and sin keeps growing at its highest rate? Someone said that, well, things could be worse if churches are not springing up. I said, "Go and study history and you will find out what characterises a 'true' move of God from the times of the apostles to a few decades ago. Read it and you will find out that there can never be a true move of God without the nations changing".

The church is not about the four walls of a building or any particular denomination; what matters are the people. Right from my childhood, I have seen Christians suffering; people are serving God in the way they believe it should be done, but yet are having hard times in life. Now in the church, there are various winds of doctrines; new ideas and new techniques are springing forth, but the problem is that the people are still suffering!

Growing up in the church, I have seen systems that work and those that do not work. Many times when I receive letters or emails from people, *"church people"* from different nations, it breaks my heart! Sometimes I cry about the ordeal God's people are going through while the leaders are more interested in building an empire rather than building up the people of God without realising.

As a leader, it is easy to forget about your people, and most times you will not even know that you are more interested in the 'ministry' than in the people.

I intend therefore in this book to challenge you to do things differently, not in the doctrinal way you have been trained, but using these simple truths to rebuild the broken walls, your spirit will come alive and you will receive direction to change your life and way of thinking.

Ready for Change

'From that time, Jesus began to preach and to say...Repent for the kingdom of Heaven is at hand (Matthew 4:17)

Change defined - *"To cause to turn or pass from one state to another; to alter or make different"* - Noah Webster Dictionary 1828

Over the years, I have realised that the "miracles" or "breakthroughs" that many Christians and non- Christians always look around for is in *us* most times. Pardon me for saying this - for those coming from my type of background, we believe only in prayer, and prayer is good; however, the problem I have is that I have seen and still do see a lot of people praying and suffering at the same time.

In the middle of the doctrines of "miracles", "breakthroughs" and "prayers" came the doctrine of the *'Superman* - someone who claims to have the power to solve the peoples' problems in a certain denomination.

I looked into this and after many years of watching, I realised that even though there are men who God calls for a purpose and gives grace for 'signs and wonders', no one can base their lives on a "Superman" somewhere. It never works!

CHAPTER TWO

Unfortunately, Christians find it difficult to go back to the drawing board to decide on what works and what does not. Rather, we are content with being brainwashed by the "supermen" of today.

'Every change starts from the inside. If you can change your mind, you can change your life and if you change your life, you can change your world or at least someone s world - Tobi Adegboyega

The Almighty has a plan for every one of his children, but that plan is left in our hands to make happen. Jesus' first sermon was on the subject of *Repentance* (change). Change the way you think, change your mind and change your attitude!
If anything is going to change in your life, something has to first change in you and your ways.

Could it be that many of the things we are spending time in prayer, night vigil and conferences for is just in our hearts? The answer is already in us but because we have been wrongly taught to believe that God is coming to do it, we stay waiting and doubting instead of looking inwards for the things that we need to do differently.

"He who rejects change is the architect of decay. The only human institution which rejects change is the cemetery"- Harold Wilson

I have noticed that Christians and most people never really give time to deliberately change some things about themselves. Most people would rather believe that something "supernatural" is going to happen that will change them and unfortunately the church teaches that too, when in fact, we have forgotten that God himself is the Author of change. He knows the times and seasons, and fits things according to the times. He never chooses one system all the way. After all, the moon rules by night and the sun by day.

God Almighty called Moses and asked him to go and emancipate his people from Pharaoh (The Great king of Egypt) and he told him the system to use in order to get success. God told Moses to "do miracles" but when God called Joshua (Moses' assistant) to lead his people to the Promised Land, God gave him another style which was to 'meditate on the Word, do it, then you will be successful'. (Joshua 1:8)

The ability to constantly look into yourself and decide to change something will bring more miracles into your life than ten years of prayer. I was once with a business woman who came to me for 'deliverance' because her business was not thriving. She had been to various places to get 'deliverance'. She had also given money called 'seed', and even been to places to pray in oils and other materials so that she could apply such things to make her business progress. Well, as usual, it didn't work and she came to me.

CHAPTER TWO

As we were talking, I realised almost immediately there was one thing she needed to change in order for her business to change. I noticed that she talked a lot, but would not listen. Right away, I knew what her problem was, when she talks to her business partners, they talk back but she doesn't pay attention and as a result, goes back to execute things wrongly which sets her back. Now they (so called pastors she had been to see) have told her everywhere that she has a certain 'demonic force' following her business. Well, I simply told her to make a change by talking less and listening more and that week she made tens of thousands, just like that!

There is something in you that you need to change. There is a pattern you are sticking to that needs to change. I believe every human has enough power in them to change any circumstance if they would first change their way of thinking.

"If you don t like something, Change it! If you cannot change it, change the way you think about it"- **Mary Engelbreit**

"Put your effort into change. Change your life and fortune; change responds to effort"- Tobi Adegboyega

"Reinvent yourself and your world will reinvent itself" – Tobi Adegboyega

Are you ready for a change?

I believe you will find a word in this book which you can relate to but approach it with an open mind for fresh ideas and direction. You can rebuild any broken walls, your change is coming. In the coming chapters, we want to examine a man who decided to rebuild the broken walls of Jerusalem. We want to use him as a scriptural example, and as a step- by- step guide to rebuild anything in our lives that has been broken. Let us follow his story.

Chapter 3

THE REBUILDING PROCESS

Nehemiah was one of the captives of Judah, serving as the cup bearer in the seventh year of Arta Xerxes, King of Persia (445/444BC). Nehemiah, when he learnt that the wall of Judah had been broken, wept and was so saddened about the state of things; he was greatly concerned.

"So it was when I heard these words that I sat down and wept and mourned for many days; I was fasting and praying before the God of Heaven."(Nehemiah 1:4)

If any rebuilding is going to take place, 'true concern' is the first thing that is needed. If you are going to rebuild your spiritual life, financial or family life, there must first be a genuine concern. I have to qualify this kind of concern as "genuine" or "true" concern because there are some concerns that are not genuine or true, because they lack the power to transform from concern to action.

Concern is defined as the ability to relate to, to disturb or make uneasy; to interest or affect the passion; to take an interest in; to engage by feeling or sentiment - Noah Webster Dictionary1828 page 40.

TRUE GENUINE CONCERN

Is there anyone who is not concerned about their life or about the things that have gone wrong or their broken walls? This was the first question that came to mind as I thought about the word **concern**; the answer I got from studying was that whilst it might be true that we feel concern, the "concern" is not yet heartfelt because it is not powerful enough to propel a certain line of action.

Most times when "concern" eventually causes action, it presents an easier and cost effective way; for example the easiest way out for a man who is going through a season of poverty or perhaps just wants some needs met is to go and borrow money even though this is not the best way, because it doesn't bring a genuine solution.

"If it is cheap, it is not good. If it is good, it is not cheap" - S.A Adegboyega

Situations in your life may occur that demand genuine concern. Remember, *genuine concern* is that which makes you "relate to the problem and go for the true solution". Concern about a certain state of things will create the thirst for the next phase. Without desperate thirst, you cannot attract the next phase.

Nehemiah could have chosen not to be concerned, because he was in a 'comfortable position' as the king's cup bearer. He could have comforted himself by saying, "Well I thank God for my life. Even though I am a slave, I am still better than other slaves." With that kind of mindset, he would have died as a slave but worse is that he would not have fulfilled God's purpose for his life, and many would have perished because he (Nehemiah) was comfortable.

TRUE CONCERN IS A CATALYST FOR CHANGE

Genuine concern put Nehemiah in the picture for change, he saw himself as the agent of change and believing God for direction. He could have said something like, "Judah is God's children and when God is ready he will do it. Let's just keep praying."- Like many of us do. We think God is coming to change and rebuild the broken walls but God has allowed the walls to break to make you stronger and when you are ready, you will find out that God has always been there.

True concern is the key to a life of effective prayer, the problem today is that we pray a lot of religious prayers which don't work. Prayer that works is built on the foundation of genuine concern for God's purpose for your life – 'His purpose and not your survival!'

Purpose, Not Survival

'Purpose' was what made Nehemiah's prayer effective. It was based on God's purpose for him and for the people. It was not based on his survival. Many times, because of what we are going through, it is easy to forget about purpose and where we are supposed to be. Instead, we focus on what we need to get us through the day.

Nehemiah knew the destiny of Judah and wasn't going for anything less. It was not about his survival in the king's palace (his comfort zone), but rather it was about destiny - "the things that you've once dreamt about in your life, the hopes that you've once had and your aspirations"- They are your destiny!

I know that things have happened in your life, many things have changed and the walls are broken but like Nehemiah, you can develop a genuine concern; the kind that leads to action, the kind that looks for the true solution and not the cheap one.

'Now Jabez was more honourable than his brothers and his mother called his name Jabez, because she bore him in pain ...And Jabez called on the God of Israel saying, 'oh that you... enlarge my territory...you would be with me and that you would keep me from evil; that I may not cause pain 'so God granted him... (1 Chronicles 4:9-10)

There is a general belief that when Jabez was praying, he prayed because he was down and his case was hopeless, that he prayed because he was nothing, but this was not true. Before he prayed, he was more honourable than his brothers.

The word 'honourable' in the scriptures is a sum up of wealth and integrity, so, Jabez was in a comfortable condition. However, his destiny was bigger than that when he got genuinely concerned, and it was then that the door was opened and the prayer was granted.

DEVELOP

Develop a true concern about the state of things. Let the concern be based on what you know your destiny is, not on your day- to-day survival. Write it down and allow it to develop and sprint you into action, asking God to show you what to do. The starting point for Nehemiah in rebuilding the broken walls was a true concern. Picture yourself as the major agent for rebuilding, not anyone else, not even God. God has already done his part, you will have to make it manifest.

KING DAVID'S CONCERN

King David as a boy would have missed a life time opportunity to glorify God and himself if he didn't have a genuine concern when Goliath was harassing Israel. He wasn't like some people whom I have heard saying that, "It doesn't matter how bad the nation gets or how terrible the economy is, as long as my family and I can afford it, and then we know God is blessing us."

I have heard this even from the pulpit of preachers in poor countries of the world, but what is wrong with this you might ask? Nehemiah didn't have to go and rebuild the broken walls; 'God was already blessing him'- He was the king's cup bearer. He and his family were alright, but he knew better than to think like that, it wasn't all about him. He knew that as long as one of his countrymen was naked, he was naked. As long as his people are poor, he is poor.

For those reading this book and have their roots in the so called 'developing countries', sometimes called the *'third world'*, I want you to know that you are supposed to be a Nehemiah for your country. Even though you may serve the king in another land, it is not enough to seek your comfort and that of your family, but consider your fellow people. Only few preachers are doing that in our nations.

Nehemiah had to arise. David did not run home to start praying for Israel and the armies. He had a true concern; the kind of concern that will make you do the impossible, break barriers and restore nations.

As a growing boy, David came to the limelight, not pursuing fame, but having a genuine concern for Israel and its people. He had the same concern for his father's sheep and was able to kill a lion to save the sheep which eventually led to him saving a whole nation.

Be concerned about your original destiny. Commit yourself to making it happen and remember again that 'genuine concern' springs you into action towards the right direction. Action in the right direction is the beginning of rebuilding broken walls.

ACCEPTING RESPONSIBILITY

Nehemiah took responsibility for the woes of Judah and the state of the broken walls, because there was no way he would have been able to undertake the rebuilding of the broken walls without taking responsibility for it.

"Both my father's house and I have sinned. We have acted very corruptly against you and have not kept your commandments" (Nehemiah 2: 6-7)

Accepting responsibility is very important; if you are going to get your broken wall rebuilt, you must take responsibility for the fact that the broken wall or the circumstance around you is your doing.

Even though Nehemiah's record shows that he was an honest man with a clean record and a good heart, he still would not shift the blame on someone else. It was possible for him to have started blaming the elders of Israel and Judah for the woes of the whole country and he might have been right, but then he may not have been able to do anything about it. We saw him including himself in the process of causing the problem(s). He did not justify himself like we always like to do.

"You must take responsibility. You cannot change the circumstances, the seasons, or the wind, but you can change yourself. This is something you have charge of. If you change that, everything will change." - Jim Rohm

"Responsibility is the price of greatness" -Winston Churchill

A certain young man came to me for a counselling session, and told me all about his problems and the tough times he was experiencing. His story was so touching, he had tried everything he could do, but nothing was working. Just as I was about to start asking him questions, he told me that he knew the source of his problems.

He said certain 'prophets' and 'pastors' have told him the source and the root cause of his problem was from his family background. Some members of his family were against his success; they were after him, to destroy him.

The problem is that all those telling him these lies and claiming to know what the problem was, couldn't provide him with a solution. The downfall of most of us is that we never want to accept responsibility for our lives; this problem exists in every race, but most times those of an African descent who have been raised to be overly spiritual. These people who are so spiritual always have some forces of darkness to blame for their circumstances.

Many religious organisations have become 'big' because of the claim to be able to over-power those 'demons' responsible for some people's woes therefore desperate people run to such places for help. Unfortunately, this type of help is not always available because we are responsible for ourselves and what we choose to believe.

As this man continued and I asked him various questions, I asked if 'he considered himself a born again Christian?' He said 'Yes' I then asked, "If you are, how come these evil forces are battering you this much?' He answered "because they are so strong." I knew right away that he had been brain washed like most of us.

We listen to what people say about the word of God but never check the scriptures for the truth or think for ourselves so that we can dispel the lies and embrace the truth. Right away, I knew I could help him, so I continued asking questions about his life and from there, we (myself and him) realised that there were so many wrong things he had dabbled into, leading him to problems he faced due to a lack of basic knowledge.

Several times, he had taken decisions without seeking for knowledge or thorough research. He said he prayed about it, and just went ahead with his decisions. His decisions backfired, and he got into trouble. He was a victim of being programmed to believe that the problem was not him, but some external force from which he needed 'deliverance'.

Fortunately, the brother listened and started to make some changes in certain areas as he was instructed to do and in turn, things began to turn around for him and he became so blessed. When I see him now, I tease him and ask about the 'evil forces' in his family and household. He laughs in gratitude. He was delivered by knowledge. He took responsibility for his wrong doings. I am not saying evil forces do not exist but what I am saying is that the first enemy you will have to deal with is yourself. The children of Israel in the scriptures had so many victories and defeats as well, but each defeat did not happen because their enemies were stronger, but because of their disobedience (which is where the enemy waits ready to prey and destroy).

Before there can be a rebuilding process in your life, you must accept that you are where you are by your doing - directly or indirectly. I have heard people blame either their parents or the government for certain circumstances whilst we agree that some people's decisions affect our way of life. We must not pitch our tent on other people's wrong decisions. We must accept it as if it were ours and move on to the solution.

People have talked about how the change of a ruling party in a nation will bring change to their lives. They blame the current government for their woes and financial crisis, waiting eagerly for the next election, only to discover that a change in government does not equal to change in their own lives and circumstances. The realisation is that nothing changes unless we take responsibility and change it.

Distractions

Anything you shift blame on is a distraction from addressing what the real issue is. If we are really going to rebuild, we must see the true light. We must stop being distracted. Rather, we must sit with ourselves and agree that we have either done what we should not do or we haven't done what we should do. We need to rise up and take responsibility for our lives, family, finances, church, nation and community and rebuild the broken walls.

Enough of sitting on the fence and complaining; take responsibility now!

CHAPTER THREE

TAKE RESPONSIBILITY

If you are going to get the broken walls rebuilt, you must not only take responsibility for the state of things right now, you must take responsibility for change; you must see yourself in the picture as the sole agent of change and transformation.

"As human beings, we are endowed with freedom of choice and we cannot shuffle off our responsibility upon the shoulder of God or nature. We must shoulder it ourselves. It is our responsibility"- Arnold Toynbee

Sometimes it is difficult for us to break free from certain ideas and thoughts that have been programmed into us by religion. Some of us grew up believing that God is coming to do everything if we can just wait and do good things. No wonder I see a lot of praying Christians suffering very much, some even go to the extent of giving money which they do not have to get out of a problem. They give out of their ignorance which is preyed upon by religious con-men who are also ignorant or just plainly dubious.

Christians gather themselves in a place for a long period of time performing spiritual exercises, hoping that this is all they need to get their life going. In the country where I was born, things have not been going on well for the nation for many years, and we were taught to pray for the nation; "Pray!", Our priest tells us, "Do not go into politics because it is a dirty game". "Pray!" Do not talk against corrupt leaders, just be nice to them and keep praying". When we ask questions, they say that things would have been worse if not for such prayers.

This makes me laugh and I always say "Go and read history again; read about other countries of the world and you will speak better next time". "You will know that God wants us to pray but more than that, he wants us to take responsibility for the change we are praying for". *A system that encourages prayer without involvement is the system of 'faith without works* Tobi Adegboyega which James says, is a false system.

Here in the United Kingdom (where I reside and pastor presently), there are challenges in the society and although we pray, we are getting involved in empowering the people - feeding the homeless and getting the youth involved in productive activities and not just simply *praying* for revival. Most times when the "church" says they are asking for 'revival', the revival is already 'here'. It may not look like what we think, but Jesus said that the harvest is here - the harvest of rebuilding the world, our lives, finances and family.

Take responsibility for your rebuilding, get involved in anything that you are passionate about rebuilding. Put your neck into the work of rebuilding like Nehemiah and Ezra did and like some women did; responsible women like Deborah and Mother Theresa

CHAPTER THREE

WOMEN EMANCIPATE MEN BY TAKING RESPONSIBILITY

Deborah took responsibility when she saw the state of the nation, the village life had ceased in Israel which is similar to what we see in our nations today i.e. people are not free to walk on the streets peacefully without being harassed: there is no more peace and tranquillity that once existed, and family life is at zero level.

"When leaders lead in Israel, When the people willingly offer themselves, Bless the LORD!" (Judges 5:2)

"Village life ceased, it ceased in Israel, Until I, Deborah arose, Arose a mother in Israel" (Judges 5:7)

Deborah saw these things happening in Israel and took **responsibility**. She arose and got involved in the process of change. She became a true leader to Israel. You are also a true leader of your destiny. You can lead yourself out of bondage and financial captivity by making a decision now to take responsibility.

"Awake, awake, Deborah! Awake, awake, sing a song! Arise, Barak, and lead your captives away, O son of Abinoam!" - (Judges 5:12) - The Song of Deborah

There are things waiting to respond immediately you decide to take responsibility for certain issues and doors will open in your life. Do you know that Deborah could have gone into her house praying and complaining about people's behaviour, asking for God's protection and the provision of food for her household and ministry? But like Nehemiah, she made a decision to rise up and rebuild the broken walls of Israel.

She could have shifted the blame. She could have been waiting for when God would be ready but No, she said "I Deborah arose"- arose as a mother in Israel. She wasn't crying to God and singing "Let God Arise". She arose as a mother. True mothers give birth; they do not just give birth to children, because any woman can bring forth child but that doesn't make them true mothers.

They give birth to God's purpose and destiny for their lives and nation. They could be men or women who give birth by taking responsibility. The very day you decide to take responsibility in the following ways...

- Knowing that you are where you are because you refuse to shift the blame on 'evil powers', parents, community and government.
- Knowing that the rebuilding process is mostly your responsibility, not government's plan or God's..... It is yours.

...is the day that things begin to turn around for you. You become happier with yourself even before you start seeing any physical change because your mind has been freed with the knowledge of the truth.

Truth can be bitter, but nothing brings settlement to our spirit like the truth. Make a decision; decision decides destiny. Make a decision to arise and rebuild like Nehemiah, Deborah and Martin Luther King Jr did.

WHAT DO YOU SEE?

We have discussed in this chapter:

1. *The Power of the mind* – Change starts from your *mind*. You cannot reach a place you do not foresee.
2. *God is a Dreamer* - He speaks about the end from the beginning. We are expected to emulate God and develop dreams.
3. *It is not what others think* – It is all about how you see yourself? Does it align with how God thinks of you?
4. *Mental barriers*- Most times are unconsciously present in our mind even through one's prayer. If mental barriers are present, there will be no manifestations. Mental barriers are strongholds built over many years by false information. You have to break them by thinking of what God says about you. Mental barriers are the *"I can t"* syndrome. This also comes from past failures that have shaped our pattern of thoughts
5. *Keep your dreams alive* – God has given us the authority to

dream; he will give you the 'land' that you desire. However, this does not mean that it would fall onto your lap without any efforts.

In the coming chapters, I will teach you how to bring forth those promises of blessings that God has already prepared for you.

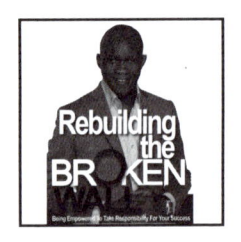

Chapter 4

THE LAWS FOR REBUILDING

LAW OF ATTRACTION

We see in Genesis 13:14-15, "And the LORD said to Abram, after Lot had separated from him, Lift up your eyes now from the place where you are - northward, southward, eastward and westward; For all the land which you see I give to you and your descendants forever."

The Law of attraction states that 'you attract into your life whatever you think about. Your dominant thoughts will find a way to manifest. *"Every thought has frequency…thoughts send out magnetic energy."*

God the Master Dreamer

'Whatever the mind can conceive, the hand can achieve. There is nothing in the world today that was not first outside of this physical world. It first existed in an unseen world; an unseen world which seems so far away but yet as close to our mind and accessible to all men. God Almighty was the one that first used this law.

He saw darkness and wanted light...the earth was without form, it was void and dark, and God said "let there be light." God Almighty also sees the end from the beginning, even before you were created; he knew you "before you were formed in your mother's womb" and had a purpose in mind.

After God had done all of this, the bible portrays God as always painting pictures in the mind of his children before he proceeds with his decisions. He asked Abraham to *lift his eyes and look,* because if Abraham could not look, he could not see and therefore could not receive the vision.

Lift Up Your Eyes

In the passage (Genesis 13:14-15) Lot had chosen what looked like the best part of the land and Abraham had freely let him possess it because he had received a word from God saying "lift up your eyes" from where you are. God told Abraham not to look at his present situation but to look into the future.

Abraham was learning from the Master. He learnt the law of attraction where 'like attracts like' - what you focus upon most will eventually become the product you receive. All that we are is a result of what we have thought. A person can be present somewhere but their mind is in another place at the same time. That is how powerful the mind is.

Have you ever been talking to someone and all of a sudden, you realise they are not with you anymore? Even though they are present in the room with you physically, the real person inside is somewhere else. I often encounter this in my daily work which involves speaking with people. This is a powerful energy birthed inside of a person which if channelled positively can bring about change and attract optimism in our lives even while going through difficult times.

Visualise, rehearse and perceive your future. This is where the action begins. Nehemiah was able to see the completion of the walls even before he got permission from the king to go ahead and build.

In Genesis 15, God brought Abraham out and asked him to count the stars in heaven and of course he couldn't. God painted a picture of Abraham's future so that he could be transported to another world, even though he was present in his natural world.

Every man is a spirit. A spiritual man sees beyond their present circumstance. As a young man, Joseph envisioned his future from his present and he was certain about it. There was opposition but that couldn't stop him from dreaming. Most times, situations that arise in our lives are created to distract and destroy what has been put inside us. They cloud our mind from visualising what our future holds for us, leaving us feeling inadequate – with a mediocre mindset. Do not agree with these types of situations.

Keep looking into the future, walking in God's plan and destiny and refusing to take your eyes off the ultimate goal! The eyes of your mind are more powerful than your physical eyes. It is 'the eyes of the mind' that God deals with most times because "man" has been programmed to limit himself to his five senses and the immediate circumstance. We have become so limited in our ability to overcome challenges and negative circumstances that we are not aware of the power given to us.

WHAT DO YOU SEE IN YOUR CHALLENGES?

Studying through history and numerous biographies, I realised that on most occasions, the same process that destroys or keeps people at a mediocre level is often what elevates others, and this is not God's doing. Rather, it is a matter of how we choose to look at our challenges as individuals.

A giant came out of the camp of the Philistines named Goliath and intimidated all the armies of Israel. All the strong men saw him as a threat but David chose to *look at him differently*. How do you look at your challenges and setbacks? A setback could be a "set up to get up".

I have come across people who have expressed their desire to be more involved in God's kingdom, take part in charity work activity or want to give more but complain that they are unable to because they earn so little; however later on in life on most occasions known to me, they end up with better jobs and I have to remind them of the desire they previously expressed about doing more for God.

It may appear at the moment as such, but if you look at things with the positive eyes of the mind you will see an opportunity within your challenge. Without the broken wall, there would have been no Nehemiah. Although he would have existed, there would have been no mention of his name for such an exploit. Without Goliath, David would have still been an unknown shepherd boy.

There are some persisting situations in your life that God allows (not caused by him) to prepare you for rebuilding the burden that is meant to destroy you. This is where you will be lifted up beyond what you thought was impossible. The way you visualise a situation determines the outcome, it will determine whether you will come out of it more victorious or worse than before.

The things you hear or listen to are also very important; many people have been deceived with lies about their situations and have believed it. They have been told that all kinds of forces are responsible for their predicament and they are in agreement with these lies. The devil has won in the battlefield of their minds because of what they have heard, but we can change that!

We can think and view situations in a different way, you can attract solutions and rebuild the broken wall by looking positively at the challenges, believing to see opportunities in all challenges.

THE TWELVE SPIES AND THEIR SIGHT

Twelve representatives were sent to go out and spy on a land given to the children of Israel to possess, however ten out of the twelve came back with a report of impossibility, and the other two came with a report of possibility. This was the report of Joshua and Caleb:

...... *"The land......is good land. If the Lord delights in us, then he will..... Give it to us..... Only do not rebel against the LORD, nor fear the people of the land, for they are our bread; their protection has departed from them, and the LORD is with us. Do not fear them."* (Numbers 14:7-9)

Who was actually seeing the reality? Joshua and Caleb or the other ten spies? The ten spies were saying exactly what they had seen; they belong to the group who say "seeing is believing" meanwhile Joshua and Caleb belongs to those who say "believing is seeing". They (Joshua and Caleb) knew that before you can really see anything, you have to first believe that it is possible.

Before you can see your walls and rebuild them, you have to see the possibility otherwise you cannot rebuild. The ten spies saw the obstacles, which was evident however they gave account based on their visual senses and not what God was showing them.

They were deceived by their 'naked' eyes and because they were limited to their physical sight, they couldn't even move forward. They were defeated in their minds. Do you know that even if you keep being defeated physically but you refuse to be defeated mentally, you can still win your battle? The single win would compensate for all your past defeat.

Joshua and Caleb moved forward entering into the Promised Land, while the remaining were unable to enter because they were obstructed by their vision and thinking. Mr Marconi dreamt of one day of having a system for harnessing the intangible forces of ether (a class of organic compounds that contain an ether group) which resulted in the creation of radio, television and cell phones. If he wanted to see before believing, he would never have seen anything, neither would we.

CHAPTER FOUR

Many of the world's inventions were put in the mind of an individual who was able to see beyond human thinking and dream BIG. They saw a *need* and the *solution* to meet the need at that particular time. Though they were labelled lunatics, they persevered in what they believed, till it became a reality for all to see. They pushed their limits and broke barriers to do the impossible and bring comfort to man. You might be thinking, "I am not an inventor of radio waves or aircraft", but you are definitely involved in the invention of your life and destiny.

You are in charge of what you see in your challenges and what will eventually become of it.

MENTAL BARRIERS

This is what I call the 'I can't syndrome'. It is a condition of the mind that paints a distorted image of your ability and self worth. It creates barriers which come from years of false information about ourselves, words from our parents, teachers, friends or even pastors. They settle in our minds and become strongholds in our lives.

You will never know they exist until you read books like this which sheds light onto the truth. This is the reason the Bible says that we should "not be conformed to this world, but be transformed by the renewing of your mind ..." (Romans 12:2).

We are to renew our minds by studying God's word because it presents to us who we are as believers living in the world, and promises life without limit. He says "we can do ALL things" meaning that we are limitless, however the world creates limitation through people telling us how impossible it is for us to be healed, set free or how to succeed in that business where others have failed. It is a lie! Break that mental barrier today and now. You can become anything you put your mind to.

Begin by searching and asking yourself, "Do I really see myself becoming what God has promised me, or do I often give up without trying and say, 'I can't?" Ask yourself, "Is there really anything out there that can stop me, is stopping me or am I the one stopping myself by the stronghold I have allowed others to build up in my mind?"

My biological father - *The senior pastor of Salvation Proclaimers Anointed church* (SPAC) is an incredible achiever who God has used to touch many lives. Often, he talks about the time his family could not even afford to send him to school and adequately feed him because of poverty, but he refused to see poverty, and instead 'lifted up his eyes' and saw into his future.

While he was labouring hard to feed himself and pay his school fees, he would often speak into his future which eventually manifested to more than he had envisioned. I have experienced wealth in every area of my life and ministry through this law especially in the area of my finances. Let me assure you this works and it is real.

Don't Limit Yourself

Be careful who you listen to, some have tried and failed in certain areas due to lack of preparation, inadequate information or improper management. These kinds of people are quick to put you off those ventures because they have "been there, done that" and failed. If it is God's dream for you and you have prepared yourself, do not fear to fail because "failure teaches you how to do it differently next time."

Nehemiah just had to take a step forward into the unknown. He made preparation but it was still a mission that demanded his boldness and resolution but he was not afraid to fail.

Sometimes, you know it is good for you to rebuild, but you have counted the cost and demands, oppositions and obstacles you might face and become afraid. Be brave like Daniel in the lion's den and pursue your dream of rebuilding.

I WILL GIVE

Our job is not to worry about the 'how', the 'how' will show up from your beliefs and commitments in the 'what'. The 'how' are the domain of the universe. It knows the quickest and most harmonious way between you and your dream.

God told Abraham to lift up his eyes and dream beyond his current situation. Abraham's duty was not to begin to ask how, but his part was to see and believe it. God said "I will provide" because he was the one who set the laws of nature and attraction in motion (what you think of most is what you become).

The Almighty God taught Abraham this practical law and this is where most of us miss it. We are like those spies who were more worried about the "how" than the "what". Concentrate on the 'what' and the 'how' will show up. It will achieve the dream and attract all you need. It will be drawn to you if you are really committed to the rebuilding of the broken wall.

Nehemiah said his prayer and took responsibility, he envisioned it, went about his duties before the king and he was noticed for his workmanship. He drew attention to himself because of what he was committed to doing in his heart. Let the dream of rebuilding that broken wall fill your heart and you will be surprised that there are resources already available for you to use in the process of rebuilding.

When Deborah arose, the people willingly gave themselves and even though they encountered obstacles in Judges Chapter 5, (they didn't even have the weapons to fight), yet they overcame the obstacles and won because they were committed to the rebuilding. You may not have the capital to start a business or to restart the business again, but I dare you today to go around consumed by the dream and commit to starting something.

The capital and connections you need will eventually locate you, you will be amazed at what was waiting for you all this while such as healing, prosperity, spiritual growth and all sorts of blessing. All of this answer to this Law of attraction- which states *"lift up your eyes and look"*.

THE LAW OF MOTION
MOVE TOWARDS THE OBSTACLE:

"So I came to Jerusalem and was there three days. Then I arose in the night, I and a few men with me; I told no one what my God has put in my heart to do at Jerusalem….". (Nehemiah 2:11-12)

'Village life ceased…. in Israel until I, Deborah, arose, Arose a mother in Israel . (Judges 5:7) 'Awake, awake, Deborah! Awake. (vs. 12)

Neither love nor fire can subsist without motion; both cease to live as soon as they cease to hope or to fear. Nehemiah knew about the law of motion. You have to set a time to stand up to the wall, survey it and start reconstructing the wall in your life.

'Stand up to crisis. Do not let them throw you! Fight to stay calm....even surmount the crisis completely and turn it into an opportunity. Refuse to renounce your self-image. No matter what happens, you must keep your good opinion of yourself!. No matter what happens, you must hold your past success in your imagination ready for whoing in the motion picture screen of your mind…
No matter what happens, no matter what you lose, no matter what your failures are, you must endure and you must keep faith in yourself... Then you can stand up to the crisis, with calmness and courage, refusing to buckle; then you will not fall through the floor. You will be able to support yourself - Maxwell Maltz'

It is good that we have discussed the other principles in the previous chapters, but there is always time to advance towards the adversary; time to arise like Deborah did. She saw the problems and challenges of her people, the possibilities of changing them and took responsibility for the change; but she needed to add motion.

Nehemiah took a similar step; he did all that we have discussed earlier in this book. He said, '*....I arose in the night, I and some few men with me; I told no one what my God had put in my heart......* – (Nehemiah 2:12)

ARISE AT NIGHT

Nehemiah did his research before proceeding, even though he only had a few men with him, he went with all his heart. He was resolute to rebuilding the broken walls, and surveyed the cost involved in order to summon up courage and prepare his mind for the worst, systematically moving towards the obstacle(s).

There are periods in our lives when trying to rebuild the broken walls requires us to be still and assess our situation. Being still to avoid discouragement from people who cannot see our vision or success in what we plan to do. They may not even see the need for it because; as far as they are concerned it is not going to work.

Being still also avoids unnecessary confrontation, enmity and distractions. Nehemiah would have eventually made his plans known to everyone but he needed to have done his survey and be ready to fight through.

You must be aware that every rebuilding you intend to do will attract opposition. You can avoid it early ones when you have done your assignment and are ready to start rebuilding - after doing all the field work in your mind and actually surveying the land of your dream.

Nature and motion

Life and nature are constantly in motion. There is always a movement towards something; both in matter and human beings, there is always motion. A man or woman who will rebuild is someone who can channel their motion in a positive direction. Nothing ever remains the same. Even when left alone, matter (iron, steel, or building etc) never stays the same way. Things decay and degenerate to a bad shape if left alone, and I believe that this also applies to human beings. *"Our nature consist in motion; complete rest is death"* - Blaise Pascal

When there is no motion to do something, we are left to decay and get worse over time. If Deborah did not arise to rebuild, Israel would have gotten worse. If Nehemiah did not move to rebuild, the problem would not only have remained the same, but would have gotten worse. This is the law of nature and motion in this present world.

As a child growing up in a developing country years ago, I noticed that the great buildings and lovely monuments that our 'colonial masters' had left for us began deteriorating because there was no culture of maintenance and motion in place to be applied in the positive direction. The buildings were always in use but never rebuilt or redeveloped to maintain their beauty.

There must be a deliberate motion towards the obstacle, and an outright confrontation with whatever wall is broken. Only then can the rebuilding start. If there is no motion, decay is inevitable.

THE LAW OF PROGRESSION

'I never look at the masses of my responsibility. Rather, I look at the individual. I can only love one person at a time. Just one, one, one, so you begin. I began. I picked up one person. Maybe if I didn t pick up that one person, I wouldn t have picked up forty two thousand. The same thing in your church, family, and your community - just begin. One, one, one. - Mother Teresa of Calcutta

Are you looking at how big the responsibility on your mind is? When I talk about responsibility, I mean the responsibility to rebuild a certain aspect of your life, family, nation, community or even the church and you are scared about the price you are going to pay; what will the cost be in the end? But Nehemiah knew how to go about this business of rebuilding. He must have learnt it from God.

In the scripture Exodus 23:29, the Lord taught Israel the law of systematic progression whereby motion has been applied, but you will not rebuild in a day, sometimes not even in a year, so He (God) told the children of Israel, "You will not get everything at once". You just keep moving and do not stop the motion; but do not put undue pressure on yourself to achieve all at once.

THE LAW OF FOCUS

One reason few of us achieve what we really and truly want is that we never direct our focus; we never concentrate our power. Most people stumble through life and never decide to master anything in particular.

"It is not what is happening to you now or what has happened in the past that determines who you become. Rather, it is your decision about what to focus on; what are the things that mean a lot to you and what are you going to do about them? This is what will determine your ultimate destiny" - Anthony Robbins

If you want to break a man, always present a new vision or mission to him even when he is yet to finish one. I consider focus to be the most important thing if you are ever going to rebuild any broken wall in your life.

Immediately Nehemiah made his intention and dream known, he attracted enmity. Sanballat and Tobias mocked them (they were agents of distraction) and offered Nehemiah something else. They wanted to have meetings with him but Nehemiah was wise enough to know that this was just a distraction. Just when we want to start rebuilding or are even in the process of rebuilding, many distractions that look 'positive'- like a better choice but know for sure that they are not always the better options. They are just distractions. It is demanding to start the process of rebuilding our lives and the broken walls, but it is much more challenging to stay on course.

"So I answered them and said to them, the God of heaven Himself will prosper us; therefore we His servants will arise and build......"- (Nehemiah 2:20)

I have always complained about how unstable many people are, I met a young man who moved from one unfinished project to another, (the longest project he ever stayed in was for three months) not mastering any of them for any length of time. I told him clearly that there was no way he could succeed by following such a pattern.

His response was that God told him he would succeed sooner than I thought. I met him years later and he was still in the same position and unsuccessful even though he said he had been praying amongst other spiritual activities.

Focus is a main key in the school of success. One key to success is to focus our conscious mind on things we desire and not on the things that we fear.

Nehemiah could have chosen to fear Sanballat and his other opponents for their kingdoms were stronger than him at the time but if he had paid attention to their invitations and threats, his focus could have shifted. Their offer could have looked tempting and Nehemiah could have seen what looked like opportunities to be good friends to 'eminent personalities' around him. However, his focus was strong through all that. His focus was on his desire.

If we focus our conscious mind on the things we desire, nothing else can distract us; not the obstacles or the things that may appear easier and not even enticement from anywhere else because our focus is strong. Our thoughts create our reality - where we put our focus is the direction in which we tend to go. Nehemiah had his attention on rebuilding the broken walls and that was where he was going.

There was also a woman in the bible with a certain challenge in her life, she had an unstoppable flow of blood, but one day she set her focus. She heard that Jesus was passing by and focused on something specific. She said to herself 'if *I can touch the hem of Jesus garment, I will be healed* . Of course many people were around Jesus, probably with one need or another but they couldn't get what they needed.

However, this woman got healed because she had a focus. This was something she had made her mind up to receive. Life will always give you what you demand from it if you focus to get it; if you focus on nothing, you sure will get nothing.

I learnt from my childhood that if you place a demand on the sun through a certain instrument on paper; as far away as the sun is, it has the energy to produce fire. What I learnt from this is that no matter how far away something is, and how impossible it looks to rebuild. If we truly focus, nature has a way of turning them to possibilities, and we will rebuild more easily than we thought because of this notion.

The first rule of focus is *"wherever you are, be there"*. Be known for a certain thing and convinced about what you intend to do; be sure that you need to rebuild that aspect of your life and look toward the need to pursue that dream or goal. Once you are sure and convinced, make sure you do not consult with people anymore. Focus on it and be there.

In the story of Nehemiah, whilst building the wall there was a time and a season when they had to build with one hand and hold the sword with the other They did not leave the work to go and fight the enemies but kept on building and were ready to fight the opposition. In the middle of rebuilding, situations will come up that will want to distract you from pursuing the goals and visions you have on track. They can be threatening, but you need to keep focused till the end. Do not be disturbed.

All the threats of Sanballat and Tobias amounted to nothing; If Nehemiah had spent time with them he would have been so distracted that he would have abandoned building. To hate is to show that you still care. Who needs that?

CHAPTER FOUR

Focus on what is really important. Nehemiah had no need to hate his opposition or show an attitude of hatred towards them because that in itself is a distraction. He continued focusing on what he had to do with his eyes set like a flint. *"It is during the darkest hour that we must focus to see the light"*- Aristotle Onassis.

There is no other time that the law of focus must be in place like when everything is dark. Many people give up when everything looks negative. They either quit completely or start another project. No! In the darkest periods, switch your focus to the highest voltage. When it looks like there is no way, turn on your focus to the end.

Focus intensely on seeing the light, and from the inside, the light will shine more than ever. Though the outside looks dark, as long as the light is on the inside, the darkness outside will soon vanish. Focus more on your desires than on your doubts, and the dream will take care of itself. You may be surprised at how easily this happens.

Your doubts are not as powerful as your desires unless you empower them by yourself. Your doubts are based on external things; things you may call 'reality' but your focus is from the strength within. As we have discussed in previous chapters, everything that is from within you is more powerful than any external force. The mind is the place of focus and when it is set right, it changes everything that is external.

If you spend more time focusing on your desire, the dream of rebuilding will take care of itself. Yes, there may be doubts around you, but the doubts are not as powerful as your desires unless you make them. The woman I mentioned earlier with an endless flow of blood also had a reason why logically she shouldn't have tried to get healed. First, she had visited so many physicians and had been in that situation for many years; she would not have had the strength to pass through to Jesus in order to get healed. What if in the process she was found out?

What if she died in the process of pursuing her dream? She could have considered all these things; all her fears and doubts, but even with all those, her desire was her focus. She desired for her life to get back on track, and by focusing on it, she was able to rebuild her life.

Your doubts are not powerful enough to stop you. Do not dwell on what is wrong; instead, you should focus on what to do next. Spend your energy on moving forward and finding answers. The easiest and biggest picture in front of us is often our challenges, and I have discovered that focusing on a problem, doesn't bring any solution(s).

Focus on what to do next and not the broken wall in your view. Nehemiah knew this very well. He admitted that the situation was terrible, he accepted responsibility, but focused more on the solution. Like I said, earlier we focus more on our problem(s) thinking we are doing the right thing (which is actually unproductive), what we should do instead is to spend our energy on moving forward and finding the answer. There is always an answer for every challenge. Every situation has a solution and the ability to focus will create the answer.

Focus 90% of your time on the solution and looking for the answers and maybe 10% on the problem. Whatever you give your attention to, would grow more. It begins to form a stronger force in your mind. You see more pictures of it because you are spending time with it, of course you will have to admit that there is a problem but do not spend time dwelling on it, but rather focus on creating a solution.

Most people have no idea of the potential energy we can immediately command when we focus all our resources on mastering a single area.

Write down a specific focus now. A written and detailed focus will help gather energy for motion. Your focus will automatically give birth to the next chapter.

loosing weight

groing up spinlualy

open my Hair dresser Shop

CHAPTER FOUR

THE LAW OF PERSISTENCE

'Then He spoke a parable to them saying, men always ought to pray and not lose heart, saying "There was a certain judge who did not fear God nor regard man." Now there was a widow in that city; and she came to him, saying, 'Get justice for me from my adversary. And he would not for a while; but afterward he said within himself, 'Though I do not fear God or regard man, yet because this widow troubles me I will avenge her, lest by her continued coming she weary me - Jesus Christ (Luke 18 :1-5)

Jesus narrated the above story to teach his disciples about the power of persistence; how persistence can turn an unlikely situation around and bring good out of negative unrepentant situations. This can also be applied when we want to rebuild a broken wall in our lives. We must understand that one major instrument to go into battle with is persistence. Nothing in the world can take the place of persistence; not even praying and spiritual activities.

'Nothing in the world can take the place of persistence. Talent will not - nothing is more common than unsuccessful people with talent. Genius will not - Unrewarded genius is almost a proverb. Education will not - the entire universe is full of educated derelicts. Persistence and determination are omnipotent. The slogan 'press on has solved and always will solve the problems of human race". - Caloin Coolidge

Many times I've noticed that a lot of people want to get to the place they desire, but are not willing to persist with the process. Persistence in a way may look like focus but to persist is what you do when you are focusing.

"Then Jacob was left alone; and a Man wrestled with him until the breaking of day. Now when He saw that He did not prevail against him, He touched the socket of his hip; and the socket of Jacob s hip was out of joint as He wrestled with him. (But Jacob kept on wrestling him) And He said, " Let me go, for the day breaks." but Jacob said to him, I will not let you go unless you bless me!"- (Genesis 32:24-26)

Desperate times demand desperate actions; Jacob knew this and wasn't going to allow this opportunity to pass him by. There are desperate times in your lives and as you practice everything we have been discussing, opportunities that have not been there or the ones that have been there but unnoticed will become clearer to you. You will see clearly because you have decided to. It is important to know however that rebuilding is not automatic.

The woman Jesus talked about was not just going to get justice just because she knew the judge or even knew his house address. She was only going to get justice by her persistence. Jacob was not going to have the blessing just because he was 'fortunate' or even divinely arranged by destiny to see the angel. No! He was only going to have his life built back again by his persistence.

When you decide to take responsibility, see the future, arise to build and choose to focus, then opportunity will show up. However, you need to push through persistently, do not drop that which you were focusing on to start asking for another task but rather, persist and place demand on that area to succeed. 'No' does not necessarily mean 'no' at the point of declaration.

'The most essential factor is persistence - the determination never to allow your energy or enthusiasm to be dampened by discouragement must inevitably come. - James Whitcomb Riley

In the process of rebuilding the broken walls, there are disappointments that are inevitable. Again, many will write down the tools right here and give up because disappointments may come from unexpected source. Well, if it comes from the expected source then it is really not a disappointment.

For discouragement to be classified as 'discouragement' and disappointment as 'disappointment', it must be from a source that can really discourage and disappoint the rebuilding of the broken walls. However, the most essential factor you need is persistence which is the ability to carry on till the last minute.

'Permanence, perseverance and persistence in spite of all obstacles, discouragement and impossibilities are characters which distinguishes the strong soul from the weak. - Edmund Burke

A soul that is strong may not necessarily mean physical strength but it definitely means a resolve to be persistent. To bear through adversity until there is an outcome of positive response that drives towards your desire.

'Persistence is the twin sister of excellence. One is a matter of quality; the other is a matter of time. - Marabel Morgan

"That which my hands have started I will see through to excellence by persistence and perseverance. No great achievement is possible without perseverance.' - Bertrand Russell

'Great achievement' to you may be rebuilding your family, finance or educational pursuit. Again, it is 'great' not because everyone thinks it is, but because it makes your life better. To achieve that greatness you need perseverance. Your quest to rebuilding starts here!

THE SECRET OF PERSISTANCE - PATIENCE

Patience is a vital ingredient that makes up persistence. The writer of the book of Hebrews gave us a very simple and yet profound insight into how those who have obtained the promises did it; how renowned men realised their destiny.

This same principle is being used today by men who achieve greatness; men who have touched the world, who have done what others called or deemed impossible.

The book of Hebrews (6:12) shows the principle of faith as the ability to see the possibilities and to pursue it. However, faith is not complete without patience. The people discussed in Hebrews were patient. *'Show me a persistent person, and I will show you a patient person.*

A patient person is someone who is not caught up in the futility of this age and time; who does not operate in the fast lane, wanting everything to happen speedily. In the 'fast lane' age, when things are 'not happening' people change direction. They cannot stay long enough for the maturity and the manifestations of their promises.

The scripture says 'they inherited the promise through faith and patience'. Patience is in persistence and persistence is in patience. Your ability to persist; demands for you to be patient. With this, it is sure that your dream would soon be realised. If however you do not practice patience, you may find that you gave up too soon and missed out.

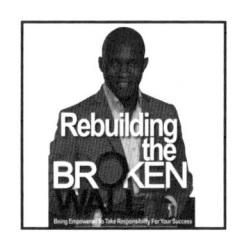

Chapter 5

IN ALL YOUR GETTING, GET UNDERSTANDING

On a very ordinary night some years ago before I left my country, I had a very interesting encounter. As a matter of fact, it was a dreadful encounter in the form of a dream; it was destiny - a call for help. At the time in my life when I had the encounter, it made sense to me but not as much as it does right now. It only made sense to me back then because I grew up in the church and my dad happened to be a pastor.

I consider this chapter the **most important** to me in this book because it is the foundation of what I am about to share with you. There is every tendency that what I want to share is not new to you and I do not intend for them to be new; neither do I intend to give you steps to success. My intentions are to help you see more clearly those things that you might know already. In case you do not already know them, I intend to help you know and do them.

However, in this chapter my aim is to let us see why we suffer and have broken walls in our lives despite our 'religious' values. As Christians, why is it that after doing all the things you do - all the spiritual activities, things still remain very difficult to the extent that you are beginning to doubt the very things you believe?

I have sought answers through study, studying does not just include reading but also watching. I have discovered that Christians and non - Christians suffer all the same and that even where some denominations claim to have 'extra power' to solve problems, the problems are still there. I have discovered that good people and 'bad' people suffer all the same. Why? What is the answer? What is the solution or is there no solution at all? Does God intend for us to suffer?

I will not bother going into the already controversial debate about whether God wants us to suffer or not. I will just say that the relationship between ourselves and God as Jesus presented it and gave us is that God is our Father and we are his children. What kind of father wants to see his children suffering? God is far better than the human fathers here on earth. No human must want to see another human suffer for any reason. How much more God Almighty?

I do not think that suffering is part of the divine plan. I think that men suffer because of their detachment from their maker however because of the love God has for us, he allowed his Son to come and suffer to rescue you and I from eternal damnation. Let us leave this here as it is…

So is there a solution to these sufferings and to the unfulfilled lives that many of us live? Is there a way to rebuild shattered walls and dreams?

MY ENCOUNTER

It was a very ordinary night. I went to bed as usual, not expecting any extraordinary thing to happen but something extraordinary did happen! For me, it was and still is extraordinary because dreaming is not my thing. I do not remember what the dream was about the following morning because it was not important to me. However this particular one has stuck in my memory over the years because the more I live, the more it becomes real to me.

The best dreams happen with your eyes wide open. I dreamt I was passing through a particular street; a street that I was quite familiar with. I did not know where I was going and what I was going to do. It was more like finding yourself in the middle of nowhere, not because you don't know what particular geographic location you are in, but because you do not know why you are there. Unusual for the country where I grew up, there was light in the street; it was not very bright but at least you could see your way through.

As I walked by, I noticed that I could hear people's voices and from what I heard, they were not celebrating or having a conversation - they were crying in agony. I could trace the voice(s) I heard to a particular building and looked at this building from a distance and it was incomplete. There were no windows and it was very dark. I wanted to walk away for fear of the unknown but I could not. I was transfixed.

Due to human compassion and curiosity, my mind told me to take the risk so that at least I could know what was going in there, perhaps someone or people were in trouble? I summoned the courage and went in there. What I saw was very inhuman. I saw in that very dark place people whose hands were tied behind them and their legs were free, yet, they couldn't move. They were positioned to sit still for long periods and had people watching over them. I did not know they had guards until I attempted to untie their hands.

As I made this attempt, the guards looked at me. Just mere looking at them made me panic, and I took to my heels, running out of the building out of fear of being captured and tied as well. I got back on to the street and they were still running after me. They looked like they were determined, not just to scare me away, but to capture me and kill me. However, in the middle of it, certain courage came over me and I fought them with words (using the name of Jesus). I subdued them and went back to rescue those I had seen earlier. It was a short encounter, but it looked endless to me.

I will never forget the look on the faces of those that were tied; the confusion; the smell; their agony and pain, which I could feel as if I was the one that was tied. They were in a desperate condition because they were just waiting for execution; many of them had been executed previously as they told me.

WHAT DOES THIS MEAN?

I woke up wondering what the meaning of the dream was. I would have disregarded it as 'one of those things' or like some people reading will come to a conclusion and say, 'it probably meant that you would do Gods work' etc. However, it meant more than that to me. I could feel them. I could feel the vibrations. I could feel their spirit in mine.

There was no way I could disregard the dream. It was more than what I or anyone else can truly understand. To me, it was more than religion or religious beliefs. I began to seek answers. At that period in my life, I had my own plans. For me, it was time to go for a doctorate degree in the United States, but I was going to Europe first and so on.

In the middle of seeking answers, I had another encounter, and at the end of this second encounter, I knew what the first one meant. I heard clearly, 'go and set free those whose legs are free but their hands are tied'. Here, "hands" signify people's destinies. People are free to move about with their legs, (hence the peoples legs were free in that encounter I had) but it is in their hands that their destiny was, and when people's hands are tied, they cannot change and do anything about their situation or destiny.
They think they are alive, but they are dead! They are dead not because they have lost their breath, but because they have lost the true essence of life. There is no more purpose. All sense of

purpose is lost. Something had happened in the course of their life to completely derail them from pursuing their dreams and aspirations and now, they have been held captive by life and by the thief (Satan).

Like I said before, this encounter, for me, set me on the course of my life; even though I had my plans they had to change for this superior plan. Why would the Almighty choose to use me for this purpose, I couldn't figure it out but from that day on, this has been my passion.

MY DISCOVERY

All my life, I have discovered that a lot of God's people not only suffer, but are being destroyed daily. They are destroyed by life; Satan and the worst part of it is that they are destroyed by themselves and their decisions. I discovered that although there are always new doctrines, especially in the church, in order to 'ease' the suffering of people, these doctrines are not genuine, neither are they from genuine hearts. The people who are supposedly bringing these new doctrines, most times are confused themselves or greedy. There is no way I can talk or write in this day and age without mentioning these faults. It is not an attempt to sound 'controversial'. Rather, it is an attempt to set people free. I pour out my mind on these issues, not as someone who hasn't got experience and is naive, but as one who believes that God has raised him not to only bring the truth to his generation but to confront the falsehood so that God's people and the entire human race will be free.

As you have read in this book, I have lived my life in the church and spent time on the streets as well. I have passed through one extreme to another. I have seen the world from two different perspectives; (the church and the world). I have read, asked questions, prayed and wept. I have met more people than the average person has, being a pastor's child and now being a pastor myself. I have listened to thousands of people and still do - learning every day.

I am not ignorant of what is called being 'politically correct' - presenting flattering lies and a set of guidelines that benefit certain sects in the building of empires (that they call 'church') through greed, ignoring the needs of the people. I know about those things, but I have made a choice because of my discovery. I have made a choice to untie the hands of people. You do not have to be perfect to do what God asks you to do; neither do you have to be the best man alive. You just have to have a genuine heart for the people, and be eager to see God's will being done on earth like David did.

Doctrines do not have enough power to set free, unless they are sound doctrines. A sound doctrine is the truth and the truth is God's Word. It is not some ideas cooked up by men who twist God's word to fit in with what they believe. I have discovered that God's people are suffering, and God has a remedy. He has the answer.

However, I also discovered that God's people do not embrace remedies because it doesn't sound 'powerful' enough to set them free from a life of bondage; from hands and destinies that are tied and chained.

Narrating my dream encounter to some people, I came to a false conclusion years ago that it meant that I should be conducting 'deliverance' for people. Deliverance in this context means 'exorcism' - that is, to exorcise demons out of people, because what was responsible for their destruction was some 'demons' or some 'demonic power'. In fact, people blame everything else for their predicament and failures other than themselves. I soon found out that the belief that I was supposed to be conducting deliverance for people was totally false. I was allowed to go that way because even though right from my childhood, I studied and loved the Word of God - the Bible (which I believe is the compendium of God's thoughts).

I was trained to believe the way I did by my mind and things around me. I have been asked whether or not I believe in the casting out of demons and my answer has always been the same (Yes). I believe in the casting out of demons in Jesus name, but who are you casting the demon out from, and for what purpose are you casting out the demon? Yes of course, we cast out demons from those who have not really accepted Christ and are not living in Him truly, like the mad man Christ encountered.

The power to do this is released to us as a sign that Jesus is alive. We also cast out demons from those who have not entered into light, and are still bound by their past life style; those who do not have enough spiritual strength to break free from the past into their new nature.

The next question we should ask ourselves is why we carry out deliverance. In other words, we carry out deliverance for what to happen?

Many people (myself inclusive) seek a change of life through this method of deliverance. Unfortunately, having watched and done it for some time, I discovered that no change of life really comes from this. Unless an overweight person knows why they are overweight and what to do not to remain overweight, the person will go for surgery and remove all the fat. However, they tend to slip back to the same process that got them overweight in the first place would reoccur and in turn, they will find themselves back to where they started from or even worse.

Let us check out what God thinks destroys His people, and remember we are talking about God's people-those who have given their life to Christ and those who are washed in the Blood of the Lamb; Those who say they are 'born again' and still they are destroyed.

I know we have been told many reasons why it is happening, for example, I have been told it is because of the family they are from so they need special prayer or exorcism to get the spirit out of them. Well, I thought that when we come to Christ, old things are past and they become new. I thought that we are in a new family and root and this is the Root of Jesus, the Prince of Peace Himself. Some say, 'Oh, it is not that easy'. I say that it is much easier than that if we would open our mind to what God says, rather than our 'experience' because the Almighty has more experience than any of us.

In the church of Christ, I have seen a lot of things happen. I have seen a lot of exorcism which again is now called 'deliverance' but still, very few of us are successful at anything at all. After all the spiritual activities are done, we are still very broke and irrelevant to the society at large. Why is the destroyer still destroying many destinies? It is important to know why, if we are going to rebuild the broken walls.

WE DESPISE KNOWLEDGE; WE DETEST UNDERSTANDING

We are seeking to know the mind of God the maker himself about why we are being tied - 'To be tied is being in a place of destruction'. We are looking at the cause of it so that we can begin to rebuild according to God's Word and not religious minds.

Things cannot get clearer than the way God puts it.
'My people are destroyed for lack of knowledge. Because you have rejected knowledge, I also will reject you from being priests for me. Because you have forgotten the law of your God, I will forget your children -(Hosea 4:6)

Destruction and death is a fault of ignorance. You do not have a problem with what you already know, what kills us is what we do not know and what makes it worse it that we are not bothering to know.

Knowledge: 'learning: illumination of mind. A clear and certain perception of the connection and agreement or disagreement and repugnancy of our ideas' - Noah Webster Dictionary1828 page 97

Many times, I have seen Christians and non- Christians try to substitute information with prayer. Instead of listening, they want to go and talk to God overnight, being deceived that if they can do extra things and spiritual activities, then they will get God's attention. But God already gave them the answers. However, we despise Gods answer and we go for a certain man's answers, so the destruction continues. *'The Prince of darkness (Satan) is the thief- 'the thief comes to steal, kill and destroy but I have come that they may have life and that they may have it abundantly* – (John 10:10)

Satan preys on ignorance. That is why he is referred to as the 'prince of darkness.' He thrives where there is ignorance, and that is why also Jesus refers to him as the thief. Thieves operate at night. Yes, I know, some will say in some countries, they operate during the day. Those are not thieves, they are armed robbers. Thieves want to come in without being noticed which is when it is dark, when men are sleeping.

His enemies also came to 'sow tares amongst the wheat'; when men slept meaning when he was ignorant and oblivious of what was going on around him, totally dead to his environment, the enemy came to steal and then destroy.
God told us why this happens. First, because you have rejected information, you can't do better if you don't know better. You cannot know better if you do not seek knowledge.

The words of Jesus in John 10:10 agrees that the destruction has and is taking place and it is done by the prince of darkness, referred to as the thief. Remember also that Christ wasn't talking to dead people in coffins but yet he said that He came that they might have life. This means that he was talking about living a life of purpose; living free from bondage; living in God's destiny and purpose for our lives, free from being tied at the hands.

Knowledge of what is available for you is the first step in true deliverance and that is the knowledge of God; knowledge of God's will, knowledge of who you are, knowledge of the principles of this life and knowledge of God's Word. I have heard some say, 'well, the reason why people are in bondage is because there are not many powerful pastors or churches', some leave their fellowship to go and look for a 'powerful' exorcist or a congregation that promises to have more power to exorcise demons than others.

In turn, the 21st century church has totally derailed from what the church is supposed to be –' a breeding ground' where saints develop and are equipped for the work of the ministry, to a mere exorcism camp where people come because they need things. Let us see what God says about the kind of priest He (God) wants and what he wants them to do; the kind of pastor God says he will raise is the kind of shepherd Christ was and is. *'And I will give you a shepherd according to my heart, who will feed you with knowledge and understanding* - (Jeremiah 3:15)

The kind of shepherd or pastor God wants and desires is one that can feed his people with knowledge; that is who Christ is and it was what Christ did. He took time to give His disciples knowledge. He gave the crowd bread and cast out demons from them but He called his disciples aside and gave them knowledge.

Have you been to congregations where they don't embrace the knowledge of God's work? They say that they 'just pray and cast out demons' without any impartation of knowledge. In such places, there is mass failure. On the best days, you have 'testimonies' but they are mediocre 'testimonies'; things that happen by chance, and in no way leads to a life of outstanding success, only temporary gratification of day- to- day survival and these are what the church calls testimonies?

I have heard lots of testimonies and I have seen people being healed of various things, but these same people plummet into a life of total failure; a life of no success or impact whatsoever. Some even go back into their old lifestyle almost immediately, while some never even left it completely in the first place. Over many years, I have also seen that where knowledge is imparted into people, these people have been raised up; from nothing into greatness, because there was a shepherd that fed them with knowledge and understanding-go for knowledge.

I was naive when I began to understand these things, especially when people will come to me and say, 'I have done everything', 'I have read the bible and confessed of my sins', I began to wonder why they were still not having testimonies; however, on all occasions I eventually saw why and the answer was because they lack knowledge. *'Men perish because of lack of knowledge* Sometimes, when they speak like that, we pray. Things happen for them, but they are soon back where they came from because of what they do not know or what they know but decide not to regard it.

Let us check out this knowledge in different scopes on the following pages:

KNOWLEDGE OF GOD (MEN DESPISE HIS MAKER)

I am a lover of 'Christian Science' to a certain degree and I can only agree that the more science searches, the more they discover that God is the Maker of all things, especially man. Also, many things that we call discoveries have long ago been discovered by men in the scriptures, and God gave us the bible as a manual not just for religion, but as a practical guide on how to live our lives on a daily basis; what to do, and what not to do for our own sake.

In the Bible, which I again refer to as the 'compendium of God's thoughts', there are basic instructions about everything in life, from how God created the heavens and the earth, to how to deal with each other and how to be good financial stewards, how to raise a good family, proper diet for healthy living, the right use of the tongue, the effect of laughing, building a good and healthy relationship, governing a nation and many more things.

The problem with fallen man is that man wants to do things his way. God created a perfect world; man polluted it to his own detriment. The action of one man would be paid for by many men including the unborn and his generation; man destroyed the earth in his arrogance.

On a daily basis, we destroy our lives by our arrogance, by

making decisions without God and living daily without God. I want you to understand that the maker of a product is the only one who knows what that product is for, and if you don't consult the maker and the manual, the product will never really reach its full potential. No matter how wise a man thinks he is or how much he thinks he has achieved; Without God, it is still a non-achievement and true inner joy will be missing.

There is a space in every man's heart that is designed for God and no matter what one tries to fit in it; it is not going to work because that space is only for God. However, people try to fit drugs in there, I have tried that too. People try to fit success in there, some try to fit money in and others fame etc.

However, none of these achievements can replace God who is meant to fit in that space. The knowledge of God is the beginning of life and life more abundantly. Another knowledge that is crucial to rebuilding the broken walls is Trust.

'Trust in the Lord with all your heart, and lean not on your own understanding. In all your ways acknowledge Him and He shall direct your path. Do not be wise in your own eyes - (Proverbs 3: 5-7)

KNOWLEDGE OF GOD'S WORD AND PRINCIPLES

This knowledge of God's Word is very crucial if we are going to live a true life of success. Again, many Christians and denominations try to push this knowledge aside in order to create and establish their own things.

God's principles, his mind and way of doing things are revealed in his Word. He doesn't ask us to read his word, meditate on it and make our confessions so that we can be religious people but rather to help us to do these things, so our life can live up to his expectation according to his Word for our own benefit. For, He made all things (heaven and earth) and set all the principles in motion.

For everything He made, there are principles guiding them and he gave men understanding to use every principle to his (man's) advantage. Again, we cannot bypass these principles, hoping to get lives built through some other means. The laws of God are set in motion. Once in a while, God will bypass these principles to do some certain things but He will not bypass His Word that is set in motion. We may try to bypass it, but that is why we never get anywhere. I have heard a lot of Christian 'prayers'- prayers that don't have any regard for what God says in time.
A lady once came to me and claimed to be having problems and

in going around trying to solve the problems herself, she went to a place where they told her certain individuals were responsible for her problems and consequently, she began to pray for the demise of those certain individuals referred to as her 'enemies', or if they wouldn't die, she prayed that something terrible should at least happen to them, such as destruction.

Unfortunately, the church has also deteriorated to that state and many denominations have sprung up just because of this pattern of practice. I asked her if she knows what Jesus said about our enemies, she did know and thought that was old fashioned of me to ask. 'It is out of date and some people are really wicked', she said. 'In this new time, you have to quickly destroy them before they destroy you', she continued. I then asked, 'so how is the battle going? Is it going well?' 'Not yet going well', she answered.

Rather she was the one suffering more. 'Why?' I asked. She replied and said, 'because the enemies are very strong'. It is amazing to see and hear all sorts of demonic doctrines that spread from the altar and pulpit of our preachers these days.

Jesus said in the book of Matthew 6:44, 'But I say to you, love your enemies, bless those who curse you, do good to those who hate you and pray for those who spitefully use you and persecute you'. Not once, but twice did Jesus address the issue of our enemies in the scriptures, yet many Christians and denominations despise and ignore this teaching. This, of course is just an example of many principles in God's work that we despise only to go and embrace other principles, hoping to get good results.

Go for the knowledge of God's word, what and how God wants us to deal with every matter that arises. If we do it God's way, we will have what God promises and save ourselves a life of misery. The next few chapters in this book contain some few laid down principles from God's Word, relating to your daily life and how to rebuild the broken wall. There are biblical principles about your finances and marriage. Do not always run and go for prayers when things go wrong. Rather, you need to go for knowledge first.

When something is wrong, put on the light in you first so that you will not be prey to dodgy men who claim to have the power to help you. When you find knowledge about it, decide to follow knowledge, add prayer to help you do what you know, then you will have breakthrough.

Information is knowledge. Right is information is right knowledge. Information is the entry port into knowledge and we must develop a deliberate information system; a way by which we get information across to ourselves on a constant basis; where it is possible for us to receive new or additional information, in order to dispel the old ones that are wrong.

I have seen people who have believed certain things and even quote it claiming that the bible said it but they are absolutely wrong. Even though they have believed it for a long time, it doesn't work for them and yet, they are not going to let go of it because they don't know better. Even when they do know better, pride will not allow them to change. They stick to the old routine way of doing things. They stick to what they are more comfortable with. Right information is right knowledge. Beware of false knowledge. It is more dangerous than ignorance.

'For the time will come when they will not endure sound doctrines, but according to their own desires, because they have itching ears. They will leap up for themselves as teachers and they will turn aside to fable - Paul (1 Timothy 4:3)
'Nor give heed to fables and endless genealogies which causes disputes rather than godly edification which is in faith - (1 Timothy 1:4) ...*But reject profane and old wives fables, and exercise yourself towards godliness* - (1 Timothy 4:7)
****Fables**: a false statement or belief. A supernatural story incorporating elements of myth and legend

Many of the things we deal with and hear today in the church are mere fables; someone's experience that does not have root in God's word; Someone's idea about how to deal with problems or an enemy that is not backed up with the scriptures - They are ordinary fables and they have no strength or character in them. They are ordinary 'winds of doctrine' that do not have enough power to transform the nations.

The impartation of true knowledge will not only transform

you, it will also make you transform the lives of many others around you. Go for true knowledge at all cost with an open mind. Do not close your mind to knowledge. When we stop learning, we stop living, as the saying goes; "the intake of knowledge is ever continuous and as you take in knowledge, strength is released on the inside to overcome difficult circumstances."

I have a close friend who has been struggling in some certain areas. Though he is in ministry, he is finding some issues absolutely difficult. Now, he has prayed all he can because that is what his ministry represents, but there has been no result whatsoever, and of course, he has fasted and has now gotten to a desperate end. Though he does not doubt God's existence, he certainly has questions. Some days ago, when he shared this issue with me, I told him who to talk to; he got in contact with the person and got some information, which has nothing to do with 'prayer'.

This man had circled himself with the wrong information and people and he was struggling because of that. He had been misinformed, and was going to perish for his lack of knowledge but his deliverance was in a certain piece of information. Words cannot express how grateful he was and now, he has discovered something he will never forget.

Be informed about God's Word correctly, and God's principles. I cannot emphasise enough how important this is, like Paul the Apostle said in the scriptures earlier, many people will depart from learning sound doctrine and true words. Sound doctrine is not a set of rules and regulations stipulated by certain denominations, dress codes or mode of prayers. No, sound doctrine is the true Word of God brought alive in us. Paul said that instead of sound doctrine, people will prefer fables (exciting stories) such as stories of encounter with spirit beings etc. However God's truth is simple and always effective. It supersedes all experiences and dreams. Always go for true information.

LACK OF BASIC LIFE KNOWLEDGE

'Knowledge is the food of the soul'- Plato

Having generally discussed how power and knowledge is acquired through information and having emphasised that God's Word (the Bible) teaches us about everything in life, it is therefore important at this stage to say that I have noticed that not too many of us embrace the knowledge that God shares with us in this master piece (the Bible).

Even though Christians claim to believe in the bible, I have noticed that for many Christians, the Bible is their religious book in which having a copy makes them 'Christians'. This ought not to be.

There is basic knowledge of our daily life in the scriptures. I also noticed that even though many Christians embrace the personality of Jesus, in that they believe he is the Christ - the Son of God but they do not embrace His principles. This certainly is a major reason why we suffer as Christians, and we have and bear no fruit like we are supposed to. Jesus' principles are the things that make us live a successful life here on earth. Jesus' personality gets us ready for eternity. The Word of God makes us wise in the world of our daily affairs, so that we are not left to suffer here on earth and helps us to know how we should deal with the affairs of this life.

'The law of the Lord is perfect; converting the soul, the testimony of the Lord is pure, making wise the simple. The statutes of the Lord are right; rejoicing the heart; the commandment of the Lord is pure, enlightening the eyes - (Psalm 19: 7-8)

When we get the understanding of things of this world from God's Word, it is the root of our knowledge because He created all things and He knows all things. When we have knowledge of that, we must understand that there are men who are endowed by God for a specific reason. He gives everyone different abilities for different purposes, so that no one else will be the Almighty but Him. This means that what a man needs, God puts into another man, especially knowledge. The information you need in order to succeed in a certain area is planted in someone who has used it and succeeded in that area therefore the broken wall that you might need to rebuild has already been built or has been rebuilt by someone (somewhere) and they do not necessarily have to be 'Christians', or do not have to be as religious as you are.

CHAPTER FIVE

There is knowledge divinely imparted into everyone. Some decide to sharpen their own, while others do not. If we are going to get along and break the power of suffering over our lives, we must have knowledge of the basic things in life. They are basic, not because they are not huge; they are basic because they are essential to our lives and important to our destiny.

I have seen people debate in a business line that they know absolutely nothing about. They do not have any information about it, haven't read any books about it or done any research whatsoever on it. They just felt they wanted to do business and someone suggested it to them. The business eventually failed and such people start advising others against that line of business. They say, 'do not try it; It doesn't work, be careful', because they themselves didn't value knowledge enough. They believed financial capital was of importance at the start but first capital you need in order to start anything is Time. Yes, you need time to find out the cost of rebuilding, time to research into that line of business, and time to find out if you have a passion for such a business.

Many think that 'prayer' can substitute for this kind of knowledge. It never does. Knowledge is superior in this area of endeavour. No matter what you are getting into, know your game. Have enough details before you get into something. Of course, there are exceptional cases that may work without going through the procedures mentioned above; however, it is not worth taking the risk of venturing in without information.

WRONG DECISION

One of the major causes of broken walls in our lives is the making of wrong decisions. Wrong decisions are inevitable where knowledge is not embraced. Wrong decisions can be in any area of one's life, such as a wrong spiritual, physical or wrong emotional decision. If a person sets out for a certain standard of life or to fulfil a certain purpose, and his or her mind is truly made up, there is nothing that can stop such a person, apart from a wrong decision.

Wrong decision is the infant of ignorance, people have made wrong decisions in relationships and finance, business, careers and in their academics because they were not adequately informed before making such decisions; they were wrongly informed or they were deceived, which is still classified as not being adequately informed. When a person makes a wrong decision, they can turn the course of their life in a minute, in a totally opposite direction heading towards the negative.

Decision decides destiny. There is nothing as powerful as decision made by knowledge. A right decision can change a person's life forever and head towards the positive. Our decision is something God does not interfere with, and that is why God didn't interrupt Eve when the serpent lied to her and gave her the fruit to eat. The serpent gave her false information. She already heard the truth and she made the choice to believe the lies offered to her. At this point, she had to choose and God couldn't choose for her, because that would make her less than a human being.

When we make the right decision, it gladdens God's heart and glorifies him because he has given us the freedom of choice. Wrong decision destroys and it allows the destroyer to do his work and we find ourselves in situations we ought not to be in.

Watch the decision you are making today. What is that decision based on? Guess work? Prayer or a Prophetic word? Base your decision on knowledge. It is safer.

BAD DECISION DESTROYS; WISE DECISION BUILDS

A lady spoke to me in one of my sessions and was narrating how many wrong decisions she had made in the course of her life. Of course, she never made the wrong decision deliberately. 'It just happened', she said. She also told me how much she regretted every decision she has made and how she would regret it forever. Of course I know that there are issues that make us feel that way, but I asked her, 'so now, what do you think the solution is?' Again, I heard the typical Christian answer. She said she was praying and will keep praying. I said, 'that is good to hear'. I then asked if she would like me to help, and she answered, 'yes'. I said that 'if the decision got you on the wrong track, then a decision will get you back on the right track, if you make the right one this time.'

If you have made the wrong decisions in the past, mourning over it with regret will not do anything to change what has been done. In fact, if you are not careful, right where you are regretting and trying to please your conscience feeding it with deep sorrow, you will make another wrong decision. Make up your mind to make the right decision at any cost. Do things differently, and refuse to regret.

If you keep making the right decisions, you will soon find yourself back on track, and that is why the next chapter of this book is very important. It is important for you to take the action(s) and do what it says you should do, and allow yourself back on track. I said to her, 'if one year of bad decision making has gotten you here, then be prepared for two years of making the right decisions, but the first decision you will have to make is to make the decision again but this time, it will be decisions that are based on knowledge, clarity and information.

I have seen people who have had decisions made for them. I know people who enter into marriage relationships based on false information from someone else who claim they have heard from God or call themselves 'prophets of God'. I have seen people who go from place to place in delusions, looking for mediums to consult certain spirits for them in order to make decisions. These mediums could have the title of 'pastor', 'prophet' and many have believed such falsehood and followed them only to realise that wrong decisions have been made for them.

I have seen countless people come to me with such stories and the solution is simple; Make the right decision! The decision will not be made for you anymore. You will henceforth make decisions based on knowledge, knowledge of God's Word, his will and instructions of the basic things of this life.

ARE YOU A BELIEVER?

This is a very important aspect of this book, and I want you to know that all other aspects will not work if this is not settled with perfect diligence.

'....And this is the victory that has overcome the world, our faith... Who is he who overcomes the world but he who believes that Jesus Christ is the Son of God (1 John 5: 4-5)

This is the point where many of us Christians miss out on the great promises God has made and gives to us. I have had the privilege to speak to a lot of Christians who claim that they believe that God will do a certain thing in their lives. Some claim that they have been confessing it for a long time and it is not happening for them. Perhaps this is your position as well.

Most of these people speak to me, looking for another way around getting their situation resolved, but I believe that this is because of the generation age and time we are in - the 'quick fix' age. The age when we just want things to happen as quickly as we need it, without regards for procedures, precepts and principles. This is the generation of 'fast food and instant communication', where you hardly hear children of God crying to God to make them better. Rather, you hear noise, but the noise is 'Lord, make me richer', forgetting that if the tree is good, the fruit upon it will be good. Where am I heading in all of this?

It is true that you can be a Christian who goes to church, and yet be very ignorant of how to make your faith work. When you read 1 John 5:5, the question that must come to your mind will be that, 'if we who believe Christ Jesus have overcome the world, why am I still being defeated?' I would attempt to solve this problem and answer this question in this passage. Focus your attention on what you have to do to walk in your victory, and to win, not on what someone can send to you or do for you.

IT STARTS WITH THE WORD

Everything starts with God's Word. For any man or woman to walk in victory, you have to locate the right word that God has spoken concerning your situation. I, having listened to so many 'confessing Christians', have observed that what they call confessing is actually putting their words together and hoping that the number of times it is repeated will make things come to pass. This is a high level of ignorance. The word of your confession must be God's Word that you know for yourself and not what you have heard someone say.

This is why it will be difficult for so many 'Christians' to enter or move near victory. If you put God's Word first in your life; allow that Word to change your thinking, and as a result to change your way of action, then, you are beginning to agree with the Word and you will be able to do what we will discuss next.

There are so many Christians trying to credit the gospel of confession (that says you can have what you say), when they do not know what it means. You must first live according to God's word, be taught God's work and let God's Word change the wrong things you do. Then, the power that becomes available for you would have allowed the word to cleanse you. But how can this be, if you do not know the Word, hear the Word or have a relationship with God?

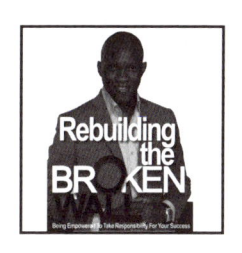

Chapter 6

YOUR AUTHORITY AS A BELIEVER

The Bible is not a book of rules; it is a bag of seeds. Jesus explained in the parable of the Sower in Mark chapter 4, he makes us understand that the seed is God's word. Do you know that there is no fruit or harvest without a seed? The first thing you need is not money to sow; rather you need God's word to sow.

I have seen a lot of 'Christians' who go about sowing a lot of money to different missions. This is good and scriptural but when it is done without the seed of the appropriate word, it will not bring forth the right harvest. Maybe that is why you have been asking questions about your seeds sown in the past and why they have not harvested, some are sincere about it and others are not.

A TRUE BELIEVER SPEAKS THE WORD

Whichever way, first of all you need to be motivated by God's word in whatever you do. You must have a word in your spirit for what you believe God for. If you are sick in the hospital bed or at home, for example, you do not need to start panicking; all you need to do is to go into your seed bag (your Bible), look for the appropriate word about healing and begin to sow by speaking it until Rhema (revelation) comes into you about your health.

Do not stop speaking the word. Remember the sower 'sows the word' and a believer 'knows the word' and 'speaks the word' with absolute conviction. You cannot overcome without God's word. I must add that I have seen many Christians who can quote a lot of scriptures, however, this principle of sowing has nothing to do with intellect, what is important is that the scripture you are sowing has gotten into your spirit and it is what you can take action on.

Reading through a medical journal, it was discovered by medical science that the part of the brain which controls your speech is connected to every part of the body; this means that the word you speak has the ability to affect your health.

Corresponding Action

I am sure you know that faith without action is dead, but before we go deep into that, I want you to bear in mind that although prayer is a very great weapon of warfare; however if what you say after praying is contrary to what you have just prayed about, you have just cancelled your prayer regardless of how any hours you prayed for.

In Mark 11:23-24, Jesus said to the disciples that whatever you ask when you pray, believe and receive then it will be given onto you. In other words, you cannot have those things that you pray on until you believe you have them. If I prayed for money, I cannot show I believe by telling everybody how broke I am. No, it is not going to work. I can only show I believe by my actions and words.

After praying, Faith is the corresponding action to receiving what God has for you according to His word.

THE BEHAVIOUR OF FAITH

Just to summarize this chapter, an idea came to mind to speak to you about the *behaviour of Faith*. Man lost his ability and pleasant life in the Garden of Eden, this happened when man fell; the curse began to work on him and affected his thinking.

When one's thinking is out of order then the action will be out of order too. There is no action without thought. A person that murders thought about it before carrying it out and this is why you cannot change yourself by 'yourself', you need God's Word. Paul told us to be transformed by the 'renewing of your mind'; transformed from the fallen state of man which includes poverty, sickness and the defeated way that man thinks and start to think the way God does. You cannot have God's thought and not have God's result.

You may ask, 'how does God think?' You know the thought of a man by his word. God declares his mind for us in his word (the Bible). If you take his word on your particular situation or need and meditate on the word until it becomes yours, then you begin to see yourself as what God calls you. When you see yourself, you cannot speak differently to how you see yourself. Your view of yourself should be based on the way God sees you - through his eyes and the devil knows that you cannot be stopped anymore.
I know people who just want a quick answer; yes I believe there are instant miracles and deliverances however, this is not what we should be striving for. Rather we should strive to get to where God has purposed for us and not living life from one miracle to another. When you receive a miracle, note that the devil does not want you to have it and will do anything to steal what you have.

However, if you will learn from God and ask him for help and make up your mind to walk with God in his word, he will supply grace to you. You will not be trying as though you are the one trying to get God's attention but rather you will understand God's love for you that He will make all things possible for you. This is the Behaviour of Faith.

Summary

A lifestyle of faith is one that receives nourishing from God's word not the world's word. A person with this lifestyle speaks what he wants to see not what he sees now and then he acts on who he sees himself as.

He knows he wants a better lifestyle and knows he has access to the father. He knows what love means and that God loves him and will do everything for him because he loves him. He also walks in love towards others, knowing that this thing cannot work in selfishness but in love. He knows the word, thinks the word, speaks the word and acts on the word. That is a lifestyle of faith.

CONSISTENCY

This is another very important message. As a matter of truth, if this is not in everything we have said, even though God's word and power is at work in you it will be short circuited. The Lord placed it in my heart to talk to you about diligence and being consistent. This is something I see missing in many believers.

'Now it shall come to pass, if you diligently obey the voice of the Lord you God, to observe carefully, all his commandments today, above all nations

of the earth . (Deuteronomy 28:1)

Being a pastor and speaker, I have seen the excitement and eagerness in people to do things after a particular 'powerful' sermon or teaching; but most of the time we give up even before we have started to do what we think we should be doing.

I have noticed that the problem is not in starting but it is actually in its continuity which is one major reason 'New year's resolution' do not last more than a few days into the year. It is not difficult to start a weight-loss diet, but being consistent with it has always been the problem. It is not difficult to say, 'I want to read the bible through this year', but keeping at it and completing it is where the problem stems.

The same also applies to any area of your life where you know you have abandoned something you should have accomplished. I believe you should know the following important steps towards being consistent:

1. *The Power for change is in diligence.* Notice the little things in your life that you have left half way when doing it. The promise of God in Deuteronomy 28:1 has its power in consistency. He said that if you *diligently obey*, not if you obey. There is a difference between obedience and diligently obeying.

Many times, we skip the aspect of our responsibility and just do the easy part. We then wonder why things do not work for us. 'If you will diligently hearken' means that all the things we have discussed in this book is not just a one-off thing. They are things that you must continue to practice consistently. If you get to this part of the book at all, it means you can also be consistent at practising what you have read irrespective of who you are.

I have been with certain pastors who start reading a book but they will never finish it. I have seen congregation members who pledge to pay tithe and are so moved by the pastor's message but will only do it for that one moment until another time that the pastor preaches about tithing.

These are the type of 'believers' who live holy only when they hear a message about heaven or hell. This is not how to win in life; rather it is a way into frustration. Such life will lack the right result it should have and such ministry will not make the necessary impact God has ordained for them.

2. *God puts a condition* as shown in Deuteronomy 28:1; I know you might have read the part about blessings which is good, but it is good to also read the conditions and the condition here is 'If'. It says that 'If you diligently'...that is, 'If' you continually obey and hearken to do the word, not if you read once and act once.

If you continue to do it daily, being consistent and diligent; whatever good you have started, ask for grace to accomplish it and set a time. I tell people who ask me, 'How can I hear the voice of God?'

It is simple. Obey diligently the written word and do what the bible instructs. If you will keep at it, you will soon start hearing the voice for specific directions. It is important for you to be victorious.

3. *Discouragement halters your vision:* This means that nothing wants you to accomplish them. Every good thing you have to do presents itself with a reason why you should not do them. The devil even gives you inferior things to do instead, but if you have read from Chapter 1 of this book, you will know that what you see in your mind is your mandate to accomplish. Stand up and do what God has put in your mind.

4. *Consistency wins:* You will never get a university certificate because you went to class once. You will never be reckoned as a 'tither' because you paid your tithe once. You will never be called a 'sickie' because you were sick once.

Whatever you are going to win, you must be consistent at that thing and this is what wins the battle. In this book, I have discussed some vital instruments for winning. When you start doing them, you have to keep doing them; you have to be persistent. This is what releases the power of God from inside to work for you.

Sometime ago in our church, the Lord placed it in my mind to call for those who would pay tithe consistently for a year. The result was outstanding. Not only because we did what we were supposed to do but because of consistency (we still do it yearly).

If you have any dream, you should know that having dreams alone is not enough. You have to plan as we have discussed earlier and have to be consistent at the plan. In this case, you have to keep seeing what God has said. You have to keep doing all we have discussed, and then you will see God's power to heal your body or to bring you out of poverty - restoring your finance; bringing you out of the miry clay and setting you high above the nations.

TARRY ON – UNTIL YOU REACH YOUR DESTINATION

'And the Lord said to my Lord; sit at my right side <u>until</u> I make your enemies your footstool.   (Psalm 110:1)

The word 'Until' denotes a process of time. In this scripture, we see that there is a waiting period 'until' we see God's desire performed on all our enemies. When you are consistent, there is a process of time. The seed you have sown will certainly produce harvest but you just have to wait. I must let you know that God is bigger than time and he is not governed by it either.

This is not to say that he will come late. He can never be late. He makes all things beautiful at its time. Even when Mary and

Martha thought it was too late for their brother Lazarus, it was only for a more glorious resurrection. So, do what you have to do or what you have learnt to do from this book and wait for God to act. *'Wait on the Lord. Be of good courage. He shall strengthen your heart. Wait, I say on the Lord.* - (Psalm 27:14)

Real people will tell you there are times you have to wait. This is something that we don't like to hear but it is true. However, what you have to know is that no matter where you are, God will not allow you to suffer. *'I waited patiently for the Lord and he heard me* – (Psalm 40:1)

He will come and help you because he has won the victory for you already. Faith is for the bold hearted. Have you allowed God's word to make your heart bolder? If you have, be sure you are about to start walking in your victory. *'We have waited for him. He will save us. We have waited for him; we will be glad and rejoice in his salvation.* - (Isaiah 25:9)

CONCLUSION

I will like to conclude this section of this book on this truth which cannot be over emphasised, which is that you are victorious already. Christ has already won the battle for you, he did not just win it for you but he gave you all it takes to win as well. However, if you haven't given your life to him you cannot do all the things in this book by yourself.

You need the Grace of God and this will be given to you immediately you give your life to Christ Jesus. As a matter of fact, the grace will get you saved. This is the first step towards winning in life. You can just make up your mind now to win in life.

If you are ready to make that decision today, then all you need to do is to call on the name of the Lord and ask him to come into your life and be Lord over you. Do it now, tomorrow might be too late. It is your opportunity for a change that you have always been waiting for. Likewise, maybe you have given your life to Christ but you know you have left the track; you can get back on track with God now. All the while, when you stopped seeking him like you used to, he never stopped seeking you.

I know you stopped because of what people did to you or maybe you have been trying to please him (God) but it seemed as if he does not care. He does care and he knows you. His hands are so wide spread open that no matter what you have done, he said that 'he will cleanse you' (Isaiah 1:18) and make you whole again. It is your time to win in life.

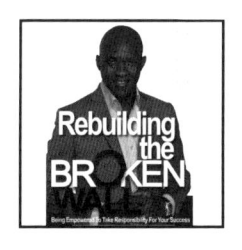

Chapter 7

WISDOM IS THE PRINCIPAL THING

'Wisdom is the principal thing; therefore get wisdom: and with all your getting get understanding. 'Exalt her and she will promote you. She will bring you honour when you embrace her. She will place on your hand an ornament of grace. A crown of glory she will deliver to you – (Proverbs 4:7-9)

In the year 1954, a substance was discovered in the country where I grew up and researchers found out that the end product of the substance was Petroleum. Scholars believe that this substance has been in the world and even in use thousands of years ago. They believe that it was even part of the substance used in the building of the tower of Babel. *'Surely there is a mine for silver and a place where gold is refined. Iron is taken from the earth and copper is smelted from ore. Man puts an end to darkness and searches every recess for ore in the darkness and the shadow of death. The breaks open a shaft away from men. The wing to go and fro; as for the earth, from it comes bread, but underneath, it is turned up as by fire.'* (Job 28:1-5)

Job, in his narrations also began to talk about the unimaginable discoveries of men; the path that man had tread in order to discover things that are concealed in the earth and even beyond. Men, through search and diligence have discovered a lot of things and as a result, man has brought comfort and advancement to the entire human race.

To search for them; some have risked their lives and some even lost their life in the process of searching out these things – with no selfish consideration of themselves. They forged ahead to search out things that can bring comfort to other men and women. I consider these sorts of people heroes, trailblazers and people of outstanding greatness.

It stones are the source of sapphires and it contains gold dust. That path no birds know, nor has the falcon s eye seen it. The proud lion has not trodden it, nor has the fierce lion passed over it. He puts his hand on the flirt, the other turns the mountains at the root. He cuts out channels in the rock and his eye sees every precious thing. He damps us the stream of the trickling; what is hidden, he brings to light. – (Job 28:12)

CHAPTER SEVEN

WHERE IS THE PLACE OF WISDOM?

'But where can wisdom be found? Where is the place of understanding? (Job 28:12).

At a time of total distress and anguish in the life of Job, a man considered to be the richest in the entire east in his days wrote this narration. In writing this narration, he considered everything he was passing through and considered the whole world as he wrote it which I consider very important; how much men have sacrificed to make life comfortable but still, in all these searches wisdom is more hidden than the treasures of life.

The natural resources that are of the greatest values are hidden far away from men. Due to the fall of man, there is nothing that will benefit a man today that will be stumbled upon by mistake. From the invention of light to the discovery of crude oil to aeroplanes, high rise buildings, ships and diamonds; all these were discovered by men who took it upon themselves to search it out.

The truth is that, you do not stumble on valuable things. You discover them by searching them out diligently. When we set our minds to search out mysteries, things that have been hidden in our lives then we begin to get understanding of who we are. Whilst it may be possible to discover some things whilst searching for other things, a diligent search is still the key in all the searches of men.

There was a man who became the 'first king' of Israel named Saul. He discovered that he has been chosen as king whilst searching for his father's donkey but a diligent search was still involved. Man has searched for many things - answers to diseases which were once termed incurable can now be cured with treatments. Man could only do these things because they searched. *'It is the glory of the Lord to conceal a matter. It is the glory of kings to find it out* - Solomon (Proverbs 25:2)

There are many things that we try to get by praying and fasting which most times we do not get because we cannot search out wisdom to solve that problem. Moreover, most times when we pray, we pray amiss asking that the problem should go away instead of asking for wisdom to solve them. Every challenge or problem has a potential of bringing a breakthrough to you if you will ask for wisdom to solve the problem instead of asking for the problem to disappear.

Every good thing is hidden. It is concealed and this includes our destiny. It takes wisdom to search it out. It takes diligence to search out wisdom. *'I love those who love me, enduring riches and righteousness. Riches and honour are with me. My fruit is better than gold, yes that fine gold* - (Proverbs 8:17-20)

Have you ever wondered why it is that most times Christians

seem to be asking God to do something for them or bail them out of some issues and it looks like he is not answering? I have heard some people ask me if something was wrong with them or maybe God was angry with them and all sorts of ideas.

Most times, when you are thinking this way, you begin to ask questions such as 'why are people who are not even as good as I am or people who are not as religious or much of a Christian as I am seem to have everything?' 'They seem to be moving on and achieving great things'.
Most times, the answer we as Pastors or Christians have given in such circumstances is more of a consolation; more of an assurance that even though those people are alright, we will be better off eventually. Sometimes, the reason we give for what we are passing through is that, 'I am a child of God and the devil is after me'. Whilst all these things may not be totally false, it is not totally true either because I still see Christians suffering. Even after all these consolations, they hope in falsehood. God wants his children to be the centre of attraction. Jesus said in His words that 'when you are fruitful, then my father is glorified.'

Most times, the reason for our continuous struggle is that we do not value wisdom. Rather we think that when we pray, God is going to stand from his throne and come down to do some big things for us that will almost look like magic. We think that he is going to come when he is ready and deliver us because we have struggled a lot and done a lot.

However, God has already set laws in motion and these laws cannot be broken. He has already put wisdom somewhere for man to go and search it out. The solution to every problem is in the problem itself if our mind is set on searching out wisdom. The people that are not as religious tend to prosper and do well most times because they have wisdom. They have not been brainwashed, 'that once you can pray long enough and give money to your church, then everything will be fine'.

Great inventions are not as a result of prayers like we use it today, they are a result of a search that comes by a quest for answers. You can only get answers by asking questions. Job eventually found answers to his questions; he asked the question 'where can wisdom be found?' We will look into this as we go further into the chapters.

There are so many things we are looking to God for and those things have already been handed over to wisdom including riches, honour, grace, glory and lots more. If you read the scriptures above (Proverbs 19:17-20), Wisdom began to list the things that are already with her. Those things are no longer hidden in any spiritual material or burdening religious activities. They are hidden in wisdom. Maybe this is what some 'not too religious' people understand.

The thing about God's law is that it is universal. It works for anyone that discovers and uses them, regardless of race or religion, colour or educational background. There is a law in the book of Genesis that says 'as long as the earth remains, seed time and harvest time will not cease.' This is the law of the seed, the law of time and harvest.

I have heard this law used in religious organisations many times, especially when they are trying to raise funds. Even though raising funds may be part of it, this law is much more than for the short sighted use. A man who has wisdom embraces this law, knowing that every decision they make is a seed, which will in time, produce a harvest. Every daily move is a seed into tomorrow.

Wisdom teaches that when you are not satisfied with yourself today, do not sit down worrying instead sow a seed into your tomorrow, from today. Today is as a result of what seed you planted yesterday or what seed was planted into your 'yesterday'.

Sow something different today and your tomorrow will bear testimony of it. Go for a new degree or go back to school and learn more. It is all a seed. Time will bring the harvest. I used that as an example of a universal law. If anyone discovers this, they will make their tomorrow good – whether you are a believer or not, because it is a law of wisdom and not of any religion.

What you sow is what you will reap no amount of prayers will not make you a medical doctor but some years of education will. As obvious as that sounds, many of us think we know it but we do not because we wouldn't be waiting on God to 'come down' and perform a miracle, instead we will go and do the right thing.

In counselling, I have met lot of 'Christians' who are wondering why they are not prospering financially. They are struggling to make ends meet and they have been struggling for a long time. As usual, they have been told that there is a curse on them because 'someone else is responsible for their misfortune' for example, some think the country they live in is responsible, what I found out was that they lacked wisdom. I knew this when I asked questions from them such as 'who do you bank with?' 'Why do you bank with them?' 'What is their charge on your savings account?' 'What benefits do they offer?' etc.

I realise that many are clueless about their finances and therefore get into debt which could have been avoided. These preachers or pastors will not tell them the truth, but rather they tell them they need to be delivered from the spirit of debt? No, the deliverance should be from foolishness. I think this is the kind of deliverance we all need sometimes. I have even seen people who do not understand the tax system. They receive their pay slip and they just cannot be bothered to query it. They do not understand or even know their legal rights with their finances. Wisdom is lacking and again, we try to substitute wisdom with spiritual activities. Every problem has a solution. The problem that comes up after you have done everything right will only promote you.

CHAPTER SEVEN

Let us listen again to wisdom who says that,
'...my fruit is better than gold, yes fine gold, and my revenue than choice silver. I traverse the way of righteousness in the midst of the path of justice, that I may cause those who love me to inherit wealth, that I may full their treasures. The Lord possessed me at the beginning of this way, before his work of old '- (Proverbs 8:19-22)

One thing that got my attention is that Wisdom said 'the Lord possessed' her before his works of old. If God had to possess wisdom before he started his 6 days work, then how much more do we desperately need to possess wisdom before we can start our life, work or before we start praying and fasting? Wisdom said that she causes those who love her, those who set their heart to search for her in every matter, to inherit wealth. 'Love' here is documented by pursuit not admittance of need. Yes, someone can say I agree that wisdom is very important; for example, the people I counsel, nod their heads in agreement with what I say, yet there is no pursuit of wisdom before the conversation and (or) after the conversation.

Wisdom makes rich. It destroys poverty completely. I have carefully considered a lot of things before coming to this conclusion. Apart from having read fictional writings and autobiographies, I have also studied my environment and considered things from the religious and world stand point, I have looked into the life of the successful, the average and the poor and what I found is that there are different levels of wisdom and different pursuit of wisdom.

TYPES OF WISDOM

'Wisdom is the right use or exercise of knowledge; the choice of laudable ends and of the best means to accomplish them If wisdom is to be considered as a faculty of the mind, it is the faculty of discerning or judging what is most just, proper and useful. If it is to be considered as an acquirement, it is the knowledge and use of what is best, most just, most proper, and most conducive to prosperity or happiness - Noah Webster Dictionary 1828

There are two types of wisdom I believe we possess as believers which is 'divine' wisdom and there is 'earthly' wisdom (of the world). The wisdom that is from God or according to God's standard is what I refer to as **Divine wisdom**. I believe that even though there is wisdom in the world, which I also believe is from God imparted into men and women who search in order to bring advancement and comfort to other human.

I also still believe that there is wisdom superior to this form of wisdom, which is given by a relationship with the God through our Lord Jesus and the spirit of revelation. This wisdom is released at its purest form. This divine wisdom is supernatural and it offers solutions that supersede the understanding of the wise men of this world.

'Then the king interviewed them and among them all, none was found

like Daniel, Hannaniah, Mishael and Azariah. Therefore, they served before the king and in all matters of wisdom and understanding about which the king examined them, he found them ten times better than all the magicians and astrologers who were in his realm. (Daniel 1:19-20)

You will notice that these four men; Daniel and His friends – Hananiah, Mishael, and Azariah distinguished themselves in the whole nation alongside some magicians. They were to be the choice men in the whole nation, the strongest nation in the world at the time.

They were to be the think tank of the whole empire and these four men who started out as slaves in a strange land were marked out for such a prominent position. Someone might say, 'Whoa'- "that is God's favour." Well, maybe but they also distinguished themselves. There was a superior wisdom working with them that superseded the wisdom of this world. Someone would then say 'ok, I think I like that. I will pray for that.' Well, yes but maybe not just praying for it but acting on it.

Daniel also distinguished himself again out of the four and he became the most prominent. *'But of him you are in Christ Jesus who became for us wisdom from God* – (1Corinthians 1:30). You will eventually find out, reading through the narrations of Daniel that he searched for wisdom to know, both by praying for wisdom and not praying for the problem to go away but praying for wisdom to be able to solve the problem.

Poverty is as a result of not solving your problem. You are rewarded for the kind of problem(s) you solve. Daniel wasn't praying that God should come down and wave the magic stick so that the problem would go away for if he had done that, yes maybe God would have come and done that for God to have been glorified but Daniel would not be promoted. It was the revealed wisdom of God that promoted Daniel. This is true revival.

Daniel continued to solve his nation's problem and the more problems he solved, the higher he was going even as a slave in a strange land. *'There is no money problem. There is only wisdom problem* After all that, there was a greater destiny in front of Daniel. There was something God has said about Daniel's people. He was going to be the one to set his people free from their sorrow and slavery. However, even though God has spoken about their liberation many years ago, it was not going to happen until someone discovered it.

'In the first year of his reign (Darius reign over Babylon), I Daniel understood by books the number of years specified by the word of the Lord through Jeremiah the prophet that he would accomplish seventy years in desolation of Jerusalem – (Daniel 9:2)

Daniel, after solving the king's problems over and over, had a bigger destiny to accomplish for God but he had to search because it was a concealed matter. He found wisdom and went into action. Once he understood by studying, divine wisdom was released which as defined supersedes the wisdom of this world. It beats the imagination of the wise of this world but it still needs to be searched out so your faith may not be in the wisdom of men but in the power of God.

However we speak wisdom among those who are wise yet not the wisdom of this age, not of the rulers of this age who are coming to nothing but we speak the wisdom of God in a mystery. There is definitely a concealed wisdom which is for those who have an intimate, resolute and revolutionary relationship with the Lord. He said this wisdom is ordained for our glory and anyone that will carry this glory must be in a relationship with God to point men and women back to God, knowing that they were elevated to glorify God.

Nebuchadnezzar, the king of Babylon at the time and all the other kings of the earth knew that there was a God living in Daniel and they glorified God because Daniel displayed his glory. There is still a glory to be revealed through those who have a genuine relationship with the Lord and not the kind of relationship presented on our church pulpits today which is a relationship that invites us to come and use God to get what we want. That is not a relationship and that is why we do not really get anything from God.

The type of relationship Daniel had with God is what releases wisdom so that we can show forth God's glory. There are hidden wisdoms to be revealed to those who search through intimately with God. Daniel had a foundation to his outstanding greatness. It is not just 'divine favour' like religion likes to put it, Daniel's mind was set to believe God and walk with God and not to defile himself with the world and therefore, supernatural wisdom was revealed to him to solving problem and enigmas.

Another great man, who is worth mentioning, was Joseph. He also solved problems as a slave in a strange land by the wisdom of God. Joseph was glorified by the revelation of wisdom. He was glorified amongst other slaves. Where you are right now has nothing to do with where you can soon be if you will open up to the wisdom of God. Form a relationship with him. As a singer or song writer, he will give you a song that will beat the songs of this world hands down. As a business man, he will give you ideas that will outwit that of those you meet because he has it all in his hands.

Whatever it is you are involved in, there is wisdom to excel above all others so that God would be glorified in you and through you in that line of endeavour. *'But Daniel purposed in his heart that he would not defile himself with the portion of the king s delicacies nor with the wine he drank. Therefore, he requested of the chief of the eunuchs that he might not defile himself* – (Daniel 1:2)

There were things Daniel and the Jews had as a covenant with God. They could not partake of some things and Daniel was not going to compromise this standard. He feared God enough not to walk in the way of the world or the new age. Rather, he kept the covenant he had with God. Wisdom will be released in times you should have compromised but you didn't and did not change the standard. Instead you decide to win by righteousness.

So Daniel won and became great in the land. Joseph also became great by the revealed wisdom and because he refused to compromise in the house of Potiphar. Because of this, wisdom was released to make him glorious and God was glorified among the nations. We are called to make God's name glorified in the nations and to make his kingdom established on earth through divine wisdom and through the display in our lives, we are called to be a 'blessing to the nations.'

The church that I see today is too weak to do that when we ourselves are still thinking about survival and how to make ends meet, forgetting that the nations is what is on God's mind. However, I believe that there is an emerging Joseph and Daniel generation that will make God's name great on earth and make men bow before him and be a blessing to the ends of the earth. Divine wisdom is the only thing that will make this happen.

EARTHLY WISDOM

'But the wisdom that is from above is first pure, then peaceable, gentle, willing to yield, full of mercy and good fruits without partiality and without hypocrisy'- (James1:17)

There is also earthly wisdom which is referred to as **demonic wisdom** - the wisdom that knows how to get around a manner that is not right. Unfortunately, Christians also practice this kind of wisdom. These are the type of Christians who have a form of godliness but deny the power thereof. They go from church to church carrying out various activities but they listen to their friends who teach them how to lie to the system and how to defraud the system.

An honest man once came to tell me how he did a business and made some money. He was going to pay his tax and there came a friend who told him not to and taught him how he could beat the system. Many people have had walls of their life and destiny broken because of trying to beat the system. He did what his friend advised and was able to avoid paying, but soon after, he began to have unpleasant dreams and these dreams continued to get worse.

Afterwards, his business started going down and all sorts of wrong things started to happen to him. His conscience kept troubling him, the dreams kept warning him until he had to correct his wrongdoings and wisdom taught him what to do.

Now, many would say a lot of people do such things and 'get away with it'. If God has a big plan for you, he will not allow you to get away with your wrongdoing so that your future is not destroyed. If you are getting away with wrong doings by using earthly wisdom, you should be very afraid because there is really no getting away.

Divine wisdom and the simple application of knowledge will elevate a man or a woman. The process may take more diligence than the earthly or demonic wisdom but when it pays off; it makes a man rich and addeth no sorrow. I have met some business men who have beaten the system by demonic wisdom and at the time, they thought they were winning. However, now everything has gone.

If you will flush out every manifestation of earthly wisdom, then you will allow the wisdom of God to work for you and lift you to a position you can never get to on your own.

WISDOM IS NOT CREATED ONLY FOR THE EDUCATED AND DOES NOT REQUIRE CERTIFICATES

'Wisdom has built her house, she has hewn out her seven pillars; she has slaughtered her met. She has mixed her wine. She has also furnished her table. She has sent out her maidens. She cries out from the highest places of the city.

Whoever is simple, let him turn in here. As for him who lacks understanding, she says to him, come, eat, bread and drink wine I have mixed. Forsake foolishness and live and go in the way of understanding (Proverbs 9:1-6)

In my study of various people, inventions and environment, I have seen a lot of people with certificates who come from an educational background but fall short of wisdom. I have also seen those without an education background succeed with great wisdom. The four walled educational system only gets us ready for a job (just-over-broke). It never prepares us for life and that is why a person can be stuck with such a system, thinking he is wise and yet not living a life of success.

Wisdom is not for the four walls of a classroom. Solomon in the book of proverbs said, wisdom prepared her house and invited everyone; those who love her, the educated (school education) and the uneducated - especially those who admit they lack wisdom and those who have come to terms with the truth that the true solution is in the search for wisdom and deployment of wisdom toward the issues of life.

The kind of wisdom that Solomon (the king) was talking about transcends the classroom. It makes men bigger than life and larger than any four walls. It is the wisdom that governs creation itself. This wisdom when searched out reveals to us how to properly deal with everything that was created by the Supreme Being so that every created thing can be at our command. Good health and healing has been at the command of man to some certain level and man keeps developing everyday by searching things out and therefore improving our health system through medicine.

Will you agree with me if I said that there are many sicknesses that would have been killing us, if no one decided to search out some things? If everybody just decided to be good religious people who believe that everything is done only by praying, many will have lost their lives and many still live their lives on this kind of foolish belief that medicine is not needed, only prayer. They do not want to go to the doctors and advised by 'faith' preachers that they do not need a doctor and therefore, they lose their life because of such ideas.

Whilst I believe in divine healing, I believe more in divine wisdom and knowledge that God has endowed men with for the sake and comfort of other men. Therefore, there is an invitation from wisdom to all men who cares and who are tired of groping in the dark to come to wisdom and live.

I am fully persuaded that a lot of lives will change if the church will take half of the time spent in vigils and prayer camps to teach and communicate wisdom - true wisdom to the people and for the people to wholeheartedly purse wisdom. This will mean it wouldn't be long till we have such a great impact on the world.

The wisdom of God is what the end time revival of the church is based on. Many have asked me the question, 'what is the end time revival?' "Is it more miracles than the apostles did?" Not really but rather, it is what would bring the world on its knees to the Lord. I used to believe and say that the end time revival is all about miracles and more miracles but no; I realise now that it is the wisdom of God in display more than ever before. The apostle did a lot of miracles and they turned the world upside down but times have changed and men have developed.

Alternative medicine have increased, occultism is also at its peak but the end time generation is the Daniel and the Joseph generation; men and women, boy and girls who believe God and win by righteousness. They do not compromise with the world. They search for wisdom and wisdom is released to them to perform better in their endeavours.

For example, they will be given ideas that will change the world if they are medical doctors. They will come up with answers revealed to them by the wisdom of God. Many lives will be saved by their discoveries and as a result, many will come to the Lord God of Israel.

The book of Isaiah Chapter 2, shows us why many nations will come to the house of the God of Israel, he said that because the mountain of God's house shall be exalted above all mountains and many will say to themselves; let us go to the house of the God of Jacob for he shall teach us his ways. His ways are the ways of wisdom and light. Therefore, pursue wisdom in whatever you are doing, it will make you exceptional and give you a name among the nations and as a result, many will come to the Lord through you.

But where can wisdom be found? And where is the place of understanding? Man does not know its value nor has found it the land of the living. 'The deep says it is not in me and the sea says it is not with me. It cannot be purchased for gold nor can silver be weighed for its price. It cannot be valued in the gold or orphir; in precious onyx or sapphire, neither gold nor crystal can equal it, nor can it be exchanged for jewellery or fine gold. No mention shall be made of coral or quarts for the price of wisdom are above rubies. 'The topaz of Ethiopia cannot equal it, nor can it be valued in pure gold - Job 28:12-20

Job was also one of the wisest men that ever lived, just like God; he placed value on wisdom before he started his work and as a result, became the richest man in the east in his time. Now wisdom does not mean that there will not be challenges. It just means that there will be wisdom available for you to deal with and to avoid the unnecessary pit holes and turn trials into advancement.

'My brethren, count it all joy when you fall into various trials, knowing that the testing of your faith produces patience. But let patience have its perfect work, that you may be perfect and complete, lacking nothing. If any of you lack wisdom, let him ask of God, who gives liberally and without reproach and it will be given to him. (James 1:1-5)

There is again an invitation to come and get wisdom to those who lack wisdom. I love the words of James, when he talks about trials and affliction; having faith and patience in the midst of these trials. Suddenly, it seems like in verse five, he left the line of discussion and went into another topic which is the topic of wisdom. However, he did not leave the topic.

Here, he was saying that in the middle of afflictions and trials, do not ask the trials to go. Instead, admit that you lack wisdom and then ask for wisdom; because wisdom is the principal thing, "therefore in all your getting, get understanding."

James the Apostle shows us that those who ask for wisdom must ask with a resolute mind. You must ask with a mind that knows that wisdom is the only alternative you have got. You cannot ask with a double mind. If you are still in doubt whether or not it is wisdom you need or are thinking that maybe what you need is some powerful prayer from some powerful person, then he said that you should not bother asking because your mind is being tossed to and fro.

However, if you have tried it all and now you want to settle down for wisdom, then you will ask with a resolute mind and the moment you set your heart to know and accept wisdom, she will be your friend and when wisdom is your friend, your life is built on her already.

God understands its way and he knows its place for he looks to the end of the earth and sees under the whole heavens to establish a weight for the wind and apportion the waters by measure. We see in the scripture above that wisdom is with God because he acquired it before the beginning of his works and that was why James said that if anyone lacks it, let him ask of the Lord who gives it freely.

The lack of wisdom in itself is not the problem but the lack of the desire to acquire wisdom in our everyday dealing is where the destruction is. That is where many walls get broken and if we are going to rebuild the broken walls, wisdom is the principal tool that we need.

A person who fears the Lord is a person who respects his (God's) word and respects him to the point of actually doing it. He sees the word of God as a guide and instruction to life. If a man has that then death, destruction and poverty will not like to move near such a person. *Behold the fear of the Lord that is wisdom, and to depart from evil is understanding* – (Job 28:28)

The Word of God as contained in the Bible is not just for religious emphasis. I see a lot of Christians read the book of Psalms hoping to get things done by it. I have also heard someone say to me 'I have confessed positively over and over and nothing is happening'. I ask them how they do it and find out that they make a lot of repetition of some certain words many times, hoping this will change their situation but it doesn't change and they get offended.

They say it is not working but that system is not from God's words. God wants us to know his word and speak the word because his words and his instructions make us wise. *'The Law of the Lord is perfect, converting the soul the testimony of the Lord is sure, making wise the simple; the statutes of the Lord is right, rejoicing the hearts, the commandments of the Lord is pure, enlightening the eyes* – (Psalm 19: 7-8)

The Word as contained in the scriptures above makes us wise either Christians or non-Christians alike. As I said before, people who are not religious most times embrace these principles and because his words are stable and universal, it works for them. The thing that the Lord commands us to do and not to do is never so that we can only be in good relationship with him but because he is the "all wise God." He knows everything. He created life and has the manual of life with him and if we obey and fear him to do what he says, our life will be better.

For God, our everyday mortal existence is supposed to be productive, such that even when we are faced with trials, it will produce strength and lift us to better positions because we have lived our lives according to God's guide to life.

'The testimony of the Lord is pure; making wise the simple ; when we come to the place in life where we admit we lack wisdom, we need to go and find wisdom in the word of God asking him to reveal it to us. Why would Christians just go and pray without trying to know what it is that God says about the issue? The things you have been doing wrongly need to be aligned with what God says first.

'The fear of the Lord is clean, enduring forever; the judgement of the Lord are true and righteous altogether, more to be desired are they than gold, yea, than much fine gold; sweeter also than honey and the honey comb. Moreover, by them your servant is warned, and in keeping them, there is great reward – (Psalm 19: 9-11)

The fear of the Lord of course is not being terrified by him as some have learnt in past times. The fear of the lord is to honour and respect his word. I love the scripture above which says 'by them, by your standards and principles, your servant is warned, and in keeping your word, your principles, there is great reward'. A person that does not regard God's principles does not fear God and most times, the destroyer creeps in to destroy such a person.

For example, God's word says not to be wicked or to commit wickedness. There is also a law that says what goes around comes around. This law was set in motion by the Almighty himself and even when a man wants to commit wickedness and remembers what God says, he refrains himself from wickedness and becomes wise in regards to the fear of God. When he does the latter contrary to God's word, he does not fear God. He is a foolish man and there is a recompense for being foolish as well.

This 'Law' of God which I would rather call "the basic guide to life" applies to every area of life. It gives us basic guidelines and allows us as independent beings to choose what is good for us. It teaches us about health, finances, family, relationships-etc and this law enlightens the eyes for those who go and search for it and they become wise and established. *'Keep my command and live and my law as the apple of your eye. Bind then on your fingers. Write them on the tablet of your heart. Say unto wisdom, 'you are my sister and call understanding your nearest kin* – (Proverbs 7:2-3)

A merry heart does good like medicine but a broken spirit dries the bones – (Proverbs 17:22)

The healing and prevention of broken bones of an unhealthy body makes a cheerful heart. God gave us the remedy. For many years, scientists discovered that a cheerful heart released enzymes which are medical in nature and it is good for the body system. But you see, God in his law has already informed us and that is why, with an open mind, we live in peace by following the word of God.

**To heed this law is to value wisdom and to
value wisdom is to value life**

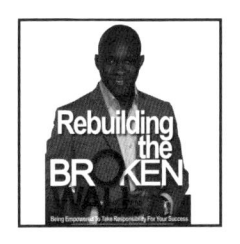

Chapter 8

THE WISE MAKE PLANS

'The plans of the diligent lead surely to plenty, but those of everyone who is hasty surely to poverty - (Proverbs 21:5)

The scripture above supports the saying that hasty decisions without proper plan based on counsel is meant to fail and lead to trouble which unfortunately has been the story of many people.

The wisdom to plan is vital if we are going to rebuild the broken wall or if we are going to prevent the walls of our lives from breaking. Also, failure to plan is why many of us do not get anything at all in life.

I have also noticed that many religious people believe that everything is in God's hand like he will do the planning and also do the execution of the plans, but even the scriptures prove that this belief is wrong. God has given us wisdom to plan and he would give strength to bring the plan to manifestation. That is why we must acknowledge him in our plans; however the responsibility is on us.

In order for Nehemiah to rebuild the broken walls of Judah, he needed to have a plan; a line of action. What he wanted to achieve and how he was going to achieve it.

'You were born to win, but to be a winner, you must plan to win. Prepare to win and expect to win - Zig Ziglar

There is no situation or challenge that man cannot overcome or that man has not conquered. The failure again is this basic wisdom that is most times lacking and sometimes, they are truths that we know already but we just don't pay attention to them because we think that there are other easy ways to succeed. Our goal can only be reached through the vehicle of plan in which we must fervently believe and upon which we must vigorously act. There is no other route to success.

Many have had broken walls because of lack of wisdom to plan before taking a step or before making a decision. A proverbial saying warns that 'he, who fails to plan, plans to fail.' Don't set yourself up for failure; make plans so your future can be fruitful.

CHAPTER EIGHT

GOD IS A MASTER OF PLANNING

'For I know the plans I have towards you, says the lord. Plans of peace and not of evil, to give you a future and a hope - (Jeremiah 29:11)

Many times, the Almighty will speak about what will happen in generations yet unborn. God plans and does not just act. In fact, looking more closely at the word of God as contained in the bible, you will realise that there is no single thing that God did without having planned it. The truth is that even your life was planned before you were formed. God plans and thinks ahead before generations, which is why he succeeds all the time.

God's plans are written and documented in the scriptures so that we might have pattern of life to live by. The truth is that Christians do not plan at all and many times we make hasty decisions hoping and praying that it should come out for good which of course does not happen.

God is the master planner and he expects us to plan. I have also seen Christians who do not believe they have to plan for their family or their unborn children. They bring children into the world and make plans as they go along but you must plan to be ready for them. God has a plan for every one of his children and has a definite purpose for them even though many do not accept his purpose. Instead, they go their own way. God planned how his son would come into the world to save mankind and he planned his return a long time ahead. The Almighty God wants us to plan.

Jesus said that his father (God) has been working and is still working; working carrying out his plans. Making and orchestrating everything to work the way he had ordained it; to bring what he has planned before the foundation of the work to come to pass; to see that his plan work on these human race.

But what would God be working out if there was no actual plan to work towards and achieve? I perceive that the reason why some of our life is not working is because there are no plans to work towards.

'Men never plan to be failures. They simply fail to plan to be successful.' - William Arthur Ward

'Life drives towards failure naturally so, if there is no definite plan to succeed through a certain line of action, failure is the most natural thing or at the best, an average life which is now vanishing from society.'

'If you do not design your own life plan, chances are that you will fall into someone else plan; and guess what they have planned for you? Not much - Jim Rohm

Make a plan right now. Write it. It would be the start of a change; A change that will usher you into a life of greatness. Planning is wisdom. Remember that wisdom said God possessed him from the beginning. Planning was with God from the very beginning. There were no hasty decisions made.

'Create a definite plan for carrying out your action and begin it at once whether you are ready or not to put this plan into action - Napoleon hill

A good plan is like a map. It shows the final destination and usually the best way to get there. If the plan is documented, if you have received knowledge about your next line of action and you, by wisdom create a definite plan, start at once and like Napoleon said even when you think you are not ready, as long as the plans are ready; take the first step because plans get clearer with action.
Take these four steps to achievement...

1. Plan purposefully
2. Prepare prayerfully
3. Proceed positively
4. Pursue persistently

(William A. Ward)

Planning brings order. It makes you know those who are needed and those who are not needed in order for you to achieve and to rebuild the broken walls. Planning makes you know who you are and what to spend your time with.

'For you have done wonderful things; your plans of old are faithful and truth - (Isaiah 25:16)

'The Lord of host has planned it - (Isaiah 23: 9)

The wisdom of planning eliminates certain people from our lives, because planning brings order. It is wisdom to plan, to write it down and to keep the plan in your mouth and heart. These exercises would bring the plan to focus; so that you can have it in your heart and be able to prevent yourself from derailing from the plan, so that when things come up that are not in the plan you know how to consciously weed them out of the way.

'Any idea, plan or purpose may be placed in the mind through repetition of thought - Napoleon Hill

The mind is a powerful tool to waste, so it has to be properly and deliberately informed as to be able to carry out the duties of pursuit and to get to the heart. The mouth is needed to speak repeatedly about the plans and to register it with the thought. One of the things that I like that God is doing in our ministry is that day after day, we continue to hear testimonies.

As religious people, we know what testimony is to us - like when I was sick, I came to the pastor for prayers he laid hands on me and I got healed or when I used to have a job, I lost it and prayed and now I have a better job. These things are fine but it is not where God is taking us. This is far from what God has in mind, but to take hold of our territory and nations and he begins to speak to us in such a season of change especially those who take the word of God and act on what they hear.

For some people, Church is just a religious organisation that we come into. Often (we) African-born citizens have been raised with an idea to perpetuate the gospel of spiritualism. We come to church just to receive from God and we create idols and images for ourselves and these idols are 'great men' who lead great congregations and when they come to town, we say 'Bishop' is in town and 'God hears him'.

Are these things biblical? Are these things the way God ordained it from the beginning? No, God didn't ordain it this way but it happened because man fell (Adam and Eve's Sin), God needed to put things together to carry man through until man came into light. Some of us need to stop seeing church as a place to go and get things from God. Some people say things such as 'after church, I can now carry on with my life,' they see it an activity to get through, so they can carry on with their daily activities. This is not the way church should be.

As we come and receive the light of the word and begin to do things that the scripture says... "Church is not a place to just come to pray to God because he will not answer you." Has he been answering? Why? This is because the Lord God set principles in motion and as we come before God and he begins to reveal his mind to us from the scriptures; he begins to show us how to deal with the affairs of life through wisdom.

Every problem in this life has a solution (don't be deceived) and this solution is for everyone, believers and non-believers alike. I found out that in the scriptures. Every single situation in your life is not a situation without a solution. The problem has a solution but you have to be willing to go and look for the solution. No wonder the Bible shows us in the book of Proverbs 1. It talks about wisdom and how wisdom has built her house and prepared dinner and has done everything, calling to the sons of men saying that "anyone that is wise let them come to me so that I can give them wisdom because wisdom is in the mouth of God." If a man begins to diligently follow the word, he will be wise.

Some people just come to the church with the intention to go and argue with someone after they leave. These are not the type of people I am talking about but I refer to those who are decorations in the church- people that need to come to church and fill the seats. *'On this side of the Jordan on the land of Mohab, Moses began to explain this law saying the..... You have dwelt too long at this mountain –* (Deuteronomy 1:5)

There are some of us at Mount Horeb. There are mountains; there are good and bad mountains. God spoke to those of us who are on Mount Horeb, those who know within themselves that they have dwelt too long on a particular mountain that they are facing. Religious people will say that when you have dwelt too long on a mountain, it is time to pray and fast.

However, what some of us do not realise is that they have dwelt too long on that mountain of praying and fasting. Praying and fasting is still a mountain that people dwell on. They do it over and over again without seeing any changes in their life but yet continue to do that. God will take you to mountains in your life so that you can see the future. Anyone that has not been to the mountain cannot see the future.

This is why God will take you to mountains and say 'stand upon this mountain so that I can show you the future-where I am taking you to.' God had to take Joseph to his mountain and show him the future and the things that were ahead of him even though Joseph would have to fight to get to his promise land. God had to take Israel to their mountain; he allowed them to stay on Mount Horeb until God came to them and said that you have dwelt too long on Mount Horeb. So what did God tell Israel to do? *'Turn and take your journey and go to the mountains. God took them from one mountain and told them to go to another mountain....Go in and possess the Land which the Lord swore to your fathers....* (Deuteronomy 1:8)

Now you have to arise, do not go on your knees to pray. Arise! It doesn't mean stand up, but to gather up your strength and be encouraged. You have to arise and fight for the land, God has shown you. Everything that God has for you will not be given to you on a platter of gold. You have to go and arise and fight for it.

There is a prayer that has to be prayed and that is – *'Lord separate from me, everyone that doesn t belong to my journey* because anyone that doesn't belong to your journey will stop you from seeing' where God wants to take you, they will not allow you to see from the mountain.

'Look the Lord your God has set the land before you. this is all God does. He sets the land before you but he doesn t feed it to you. (Deuteronomy 1:21) The specific land that God has destined for you could be in any area of your life such as your family, finances or business. There is a land that God has set before you but he won't give it to you till you arise and take it. Go and possess it without being afraid or discouraged.

God is saying that we should get out of our comfort zone and compliance. The children of Israel were stuck between their job and their dreams and this is what happens to us in the United Kingdom. People are stuck between their job (Just over broke) and their dream and it becomes impossible for you to press into the desire and the will of God for you life. This is why people are stuck in the same job for 15 to 20 years saying that it is paying their mortgage. They are on their Mount Horeb and God keeps speaking to them but they are afraid to come down. He says that there are new lands to possess and new steps for them to take but there is fear in them. They keep thinking that if I cannot go forward, I'd rather stay where I am; in my comfort zone.

They say that 'with my age now, I cannot do anything else.' However, there was a man called Caleb who at the age of 85, spoke to Joshua and was able to possess the land. Caleb was still conquering new territories at this prime age. But the beginning of every movement from Mount Horeb is to take the first step.

Many of us in this country are stuck between our job and our dream. We don't have courage to take new territories. You need to arise and say "you believe that you are well able to possess the land and go after your dreams."

'You need to depart from Mount Horeb and go and possess the land of the Amorites.'...*Go and engage him in battle....* – (Deuteronomy 2:24)

'You take the first step without knowing the second step - Martin Luther King Jr.

God is not going to arise and fight for you. You need to face your fear and those things that say to you that you cannot possess the land - engage it in battle. The problem with many of us is that we believe that we are never going to amount to anything. Do not let any pastor deceive you that you should just be praying, saying that our God is a 'God of breakthrough'.

Our God is a God that asks you to arise and engage your obstacle in battle. Begin to envision new territories in your mind and do not view the challenges as a demonic problem. There is no one single mention of demons in the bible - old testament. The only person that is mentioned as a demon was an angel who was talking about the prince of Persia.

God is too big to be trying to fight demons for you. I, in my own little capacity already think that I am much more bigger than any demon not to talk of the Almighty God and I do not spend time binding them and praying against them. God knows that there are mountains; he knows that there are things in your life and he gives us the tactics of how to deal with them. Even though Moses was a child of promise and was the one that brought Israel out of Egypt, he said that if you do not go and engage in battle, you still won't possess the land.

Is there any thing in your life that you are going to engage in battle with? Is there anything that you are pressing forward into, saying that I am not going to stay on this mountain anymore?' It is a battle! *'Lord open my eyes to see that I am getting bigger than my mountains.* (vs. 25) Have you ever seen a mountain that grows bigger? Your mountains do not get bigger. You only get smaller therefore it seems that your problems are over shadowing you. You have the capacity to grow bigger than your mountain.

There is a mountain that I have been to a few times and since I left, I heard that it has not grown an inch. The only reason why your mountain is not diminishing is because you are not growing. You are not getting bigger and the intention of God is to make you bigger than your mountain; you get bigger by engaging the mountain in battle not by crying or being fearful. Crying only makes you look smaller than the mountain.

Goliath was standing on the mountain and threatening the children of Israel and a small boy David who knew the Lord his God was not going to go back home and say, 'well, the only thing we can be doing for Israel is prayer so I will go back home to pray and gather Israel for a free prayer conference'. This is what we Christians do.

The country where I grew up became 50 years in existence in 2010; you can hardly find five pastors who speak against the evil of the society but rather they are getting wealthier (buying jets) through illegitimate money. We need people who will speak out against the bad norms and evils of the community; the church is the hope of the whole nation; others go looking for camps because a great preacher is in town…they start saying a great prayer for Nigeria.

When I was in Ukraine, a certain pastor will go out on the street carrying bill boards protesting to engage the mountain in battle until the mountain is subdued before us and the nations is brought on its kneels. Do know what prosperity means to the pastors in my country? They say that 'it doesn't matter how much they sell things in our country, so long as other people in my church can buy it that means that we are prospering'. This is not **prospering**.

They are 'prospering' but you are not.

Do not run back to your closet and say 'Pastor, I am just praying and I will be still until when God is ready'. No! This should not be so. You need to be ready to leave Horeb. When you are ready to leave the place of mediocrity and snap out of complacency, ready to say that 'I know for sure that God has already won the battle for me, it is time for me to arise. I am going to possess the land; I am not going to be stuck between my job and my dreams. I will rather pursue my dream and die in the middle of it than sit down on Mount Horeb.'

There is a problem in this country as I look into your eyes, I can see the problem staring me in my face and that is complacency and your comfort zone; you get so comfortable that you are not willing to take new territories any more. You are not willing to do new things or willing to engage in new tasks anymore. The issue is that you are not really comfortable now because what you call 'comfort' is actually 'poverty.' The children of Israel were protected in Mount Horeb but God had more in mind for them. They departed from Horeb and then they came to a place called Kadasbanare (a place of compromise).

In the middle of arising and moving, compromise comes in whereby you begin to get scared and afraid, what if it doesn't work. There will be so many '**what ifs**'; 'what about my family and my children?' 'Do I go back or do I go forward?' You will get to a place in your life where compromise is no longer an option.

'If a man has not found something worth living for, the man is not fit to live.'-Martin Luther King Jr.

If you haven't found something that you will live and die for, then life is not worth living. I will die for the way I talk and I laugh when people try and correct me. If you haven't found what to live for, that man is not fit to be alive. God's arrangement would have been concluded for you but if you cannot arise and possess it, you cannot have it. David took Goliath by surprise. Goliath represents the mountain against Israel and the best thing David could have done as a "good Christian" in the 21st century and simply organise a prayer group/camp - he will be praying in the camp and Goliath would be killing his people like ants. Just like many of us, he will come back and ask, 'Does God really exist because I do not know what is going on in my life?' Yes, God really does exist. God will not just act until you act, he will not arise until you arise and he will not fight until you fight.

The Bible says that David ran towards Goliath, he engaged Goliath in a battle and he wasn't going to call for any reinforcement. He was ready to fight. Goliath would have been thinking and looking at David as an ant but David had another tactic. One of the things that David did was that he planned for the battle and he was prepared for the battle. Many Christians don't plan but rather we say that everything is in the hands of God.

I had a Pastor tell me that you don't need to plan and that every plan is with God. God Almighty himself plans. He said in Jeremiah 29:11 he says, 'I know the plans, I have towards you.' Before God formed you, he had planned your life, but it is up to you to discover it and make preparation to overcome the battles in your life in partnership with God.

A young man was telling me that he had already started to plan for the next year in Autumn of the previous year and I said that you are becoming a real Christian. Some people only start to plan for the New Year on the 31st of December, calling it their New Year resolution which only lasts for two weeks before they give up on what they had planned. For every territory that you want to take, there are enemies around who will try to stop you but don't let anyone deceive you that it is the cause of a generational curse or something.

The world by itself is a battle field. Whether you have demons in your dad's house or your mum's house, it really does not matter. If you are really going to possess anything, there are powers and forces to contest with and some of the forces are just natural laws. You have to contend and engage them in battle if not you will not move from Horeb to the Mountain of the Amorites.

SNAP OUT OF COMPLACENCY

Lethargy is the 'quality or state of being drowsy 'when there is no energy and your energy is not based on the capital you have. There is no business venture in the world that starts with capital, it starts with vision. When the vision is right, the law of attraction will attract the things that you need to you. Go and write down new things that you want to do, new lands that you want to take. Sometimes it will take years to possess the land but you have to have a dream and plan to possess the land and you need to have courage to go and possess that land.

The word of God is the only hope we have for those that listen. If you go and pray without knowing what God is saying, it looks to you as if God does not exist. You start to ask, 'Where is God in all this? The world is prospering but we are not because God sets principles in motion that Christians do not bother to want to know but we would rather pray and fast. After fasting, things still do not happen.

Proverbs 4 says 'Wisdom is the principle thing.' There is nothing called "money problem", there is a "wisdom problem". For every problem, there is a certain solution and prayer is not the only solution. I do not fear religious option however some religious people's hearts are closed. They cannot go back and review the things that they have done in the past and see that it is not working and change what they do.

I am a man given to pray by the grace of God but I know what prayer is supposed to do and what prayer will never do. For some of us, if we are to gauge our prosperity with how much we pray, we should be richer than Donald trump and I doubt whether he prays at all. Christians are the most foolish set of people on earth including me and you because we are tricked. We have believed wrongly and God is saying that we should snap out of complacency.

For some people, the mountain where they have dwelt on is the mountain on prayer. In the country where I grew up, they have what we call 'revival' but the nation is very sick but there is no single person that will rise up against the evil yet they say there is revival. The church is big but yet there is nothing to show for it in the nation but there is a new generation. '*The LORD our God spake unto us in Horeb, saying, Ye have dwelt long enough in this mount –* (Deuteronomy 1:6)

The churches in our nation sit down in their four walls saying that we are praying but they stay in the place of prayer and do nothing. With all your prayers, nothing changes in your life because God has said that it is time for you to 'Arise, Go and Possess the land because he has already given it to you.'
The things that you think are holding you down are not as powerful as you think they are. What you perceive as your problem is programmed to discourage you from engaging the problem in a battle in the first place. There is no power - powerful enough to deliver you from where way your mind goes.

There are things in your life and people in your life that without them leaving, you will not be able to move forward in life. You should ask God to separate you from people that are not supposed to be in your destiny. You must know the purpose for everything that you pass through; God had to shut the womb of Hannah or Sarah in order to open the womb of a nation. Search the will of God and let him lead you in the right path.

Have you noticed that all the three patriarchs of faith, had their wombs shut because God did not intend them to have just sons but to bring forth nations? God told us to occupy till he comes not just to fill up but we need to occupy, possess and conquer new territories. Start doing new things with your life. Remember Caleb at the age of 85 was ready to conquer new territories. Age is calculated in exploits not in numbers.

I respect age but it is not calculated in numbers but by how many lives you have touched. The purpose of God for your life is for you to exist but to touch somebody else and you must see your tithe as part of this blessing. Many Christians still carry the word of God that has not become flesh. The word becomes flesh when people can see the word of God in operation in your life.

The book of Deuteronomy Chapter 2 shows that people will try out something a few times and give up with the conclusion that something is not right. Every meaningful invention in the world, at the point of breakthrough after the invention was tried more than a hundred times. One word God told me was that 'The Word of God became flesh.' The word of God in your life that becomes flesh is the practicality of the word that you hear every day and not in your spirituality.

The word became flesh in that they can see the word in operation in your life and you are engaging your enemies constantly. A man who knows who they are is ten times more powerful than Satan....where did we get our kind of Christianity from that always talks about demons and Satan?

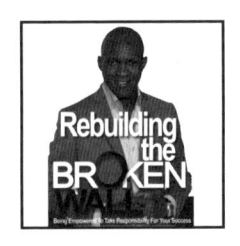

Chapter 9

AFTER ALL IS SAID AND DONE

Now, it is YOUR time to rebuild.

'Then Eliashib the high priest rose up with his brethren the priest and built the steep gate - Nehemiah 3:1

I will like to start this concluding part by emphasising on the quote above. The time is always right to do what is right. The wall that needs to be rebuilt is your life or nation. Have you considered it right? Have you looked around, thought about your circumstances and your society and have you noticed that there is still something to rebuild? If your answer is yes, then again, 'the time is always right to do what is right'.

CHAPTER NINE

'Change does not roll in on the wheels of inevitability, but comes through continuous struggle. And so we must straighten our backs and work for our freedom. A man cannot ride unless your back is bent'. Martin Luther King Jr

Dr King was talking in the context of rebuilding a nation that was once founded on the pillars of justice and equality. I am also speaking in this context and also bringing these principles into rebuilding our broken walls in our lives.

'The time is always right to do what is right' - Martin Luther King Jr

The ability to rise up once having learnt the principles of rebuilding shows that we believe we can rebuild and that we are willing to struggle until we see the changes we desire and become who we really want to be. Never try to wait till tomorrow in order to do what you know is right.

The rebuilding of the wall is your destiny. You are holding this book because you are destined to do something extraordinary with the principles you have learnt. Taking the first step(s) is going to bring you inner joy and bring fulfilment to your life.
The following steps are the beginning to experiencing a solid foundation of your broken walls:

1. DIVINE VISITATIONS:

At various times, the Almighty according to the scriptures has 'visited' mortal men. Growing up in the church and listening to preachers, I have always had the notion of divine visitation being something very spiritual and when God comes 'visiting', they say he comes to bless whoever is being visited. They say things like, 'when you are barren as a woman, and God comes visiting then you will have a baby'; 'when you are sick and God comes visiting, then you will be healed' etc. However, as I began to study the act of God, I understood that divine visitation is very real.

God does visit mortal men in various ways; in ways that the person being visited can understand. He communicates with men in their own language, but the difference is that he doesn't come to give man what will bring him immediate gratification(s), the way I was taught, but rather, he comes to send us on an assignment- to rebuild the lives of others. I saw this clearly in the scriptures which makes me wonder sometimes what exactly our preachers are reading.

We saw in the scriptures a man called Noah and what we can refer to as a divine visitation. God wanted this man to build an ark; an Ark which was supposed to be for the saving of the world. He gave him an assignment, a responsibility for Noah to carry out; for his (Noah's) generation.

CHAPTER NINE

Going further into the scripture, we will find another man named Abraham. Abraham at the time had an encounter with God where he was asked to leave his father's house and country home to a land that would be revealed to him.

There, he would become what God wanted him to be - which was the 'father of all nations'; from the time of this visitation he was going to become a sojourner. He had an assignment and responsibility to take upon himself in his generation (you will see Abraham's visitation in Genesis 12).

Again, we saw another man called Moses. He had an encounter in Exodus chapter 3. This visitation is popularly known as the 'burning bush' encounter and this also came to give him a responsibility to rebuild the life of his nation; to bring people out of bondage and speak on behalf of God for the liberation of his people. Whether in a burning bush or a conscience that was steered by justice or from Noah to Dr Martin Luther King or within our present generation, there is still a divine visitation. Are visitations steering us up? Are they saying to us that now, it is time to rebuild the broken walls of our life?

Remember that at the time that Abraham had a divine visitation, he was of advanced age and yet he was without child. He and his wife Sarah were barren and one would have thought 'God was coming to give him a child', but no, God came to give him a responsibility; a responsibility because he was not just going to be the father of one child, but the father of many nations.

Your decisions to rise up today and start rebuilding can end up in greatness you've never imagined.

2. ARISE AND BUILD

'Arise; shine; for your light has come! And the glory of the Lord is rise upon you - (Isaiah 60:1) This scripture of Isaiah charges us to arise and shine, I have always heard this as a 'prophetic' bible sermon but whilst I do not dispute this, I think it is deeper than that. The writer Isaiah went further to tell us why he said 'Arise and Shine because your light has come'.

Light here stands for illumination, clarity, knowledge, foresight, hope and direction. I believe that through the principles shared in this book, there is light for you. Your light has come and he (Isaiah) therefore says that once there is light, you have to arise. Once there is clarity about what to rebuild and why it should be rebuilt, then it is left to you to arise. Once you arise, you will definitely shine.

'Change happens because ordinary people decide to do extraordinary things' -Martin Luther King Jr

A certain king in Israel discovered at the age of eight what it takes to rebuild the temple of the Lord. He found out the book of the Law in the ruins of the temple and this marked the beginning of his shining because King Josiah discovered how to rebuild and he therefore became a shining light due to his decision. He was an ordinary king who decided to do something extraordinary. He wasn't held back by how badly the walls had been broken but was inspired by the end result of rebuilding and like Nehemiah, he endured all resistance because of the glory that would surge forth when the broken walls has been rebuilt. There is a glory waiting at the point of your decision to rebuild the broken walls.

3. GO TO THE MOUNTAIN TOP

On the mountain top, you are able to see from a far distance. One of the most powerful speeches ever given by Dr Martin Luther King Jr was given a night before he was murdered and it was titled, *'I have been to the mountain top*. In this speech, Dr King emphasised that he already sees the end of their struggle as people of colour in America. He said he already sees what he called 'the promised land'. He was saying all these in the middle of their struggle for emancipation.

As you begin to put one brick on another, trying to rebuild the broken walls(s), take yourself again and again to the mountain top and never allow the picture of the mountain top to leave you as you rebuild the broken wall(s). This mountain top picture will help you visualise your success through the inevitable struggle involved in rebuilding the broken walls.

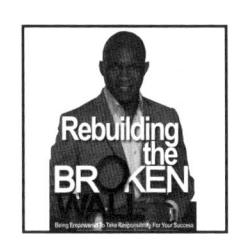

Chapter 10

HOW LONG WILL IT TAKE? NOT LONG!

No matter how frustrating the hour may be or how hopeless the situation of the broken wall(s) in your life or nation might be, it will not be long till you rebuild the broken wall. If you are asking questions today having read through this book, you are asking, 'How long?', 'How long will I be restored?' or How long will it take to get back to where I really want to be?'

I say to you today, 'not too long' because you have decided to arise and rebuild. It won't be long because you have decided to confront the issues and have refused to fear or be discouraged. You have seen the possibility and the Promised Land from the mountain top, therefore it shouldn't be long till the walls of Jerusalem will be rebuilt or your family restored again. It will not be long till we see our nations back to the original plan of God for the nations.

Our nations will again be built on the pillars of justice and equality. 'Developing countries' of Africa will rise again in integrity and dignity. You have an assignment for your life and for the nations. Life is never really about us but if you decide to make your life work and successful by rebuilding the broken walls, you will be helping many others along the way to fulfill their destiny.

I have chosen to look at every decision I make; as decisions that will either bless or ruin lives and because of this, I have decided to live a life of true success. True success is based on how many lives my existence and life has touched through providing help, inspiration, direction and motivation too. The day Nehemiah decided to rebuild the broken wall, he made a decision to bring solace to the life of many including unborn children.

The day you decide to rebuild any broken wall(s) in your life means you just made a decision to be a blessing to yourself and many others. Thank God for great liberators in past generations whose names still exist even though they have departed from the world years ago. Their memory stays on earth because they were builders.

Today, make a decision to rebuild and build so you can leave a mark on earth that will never be erased. You will also have an eternal reward from God the creator. How long? It won't be long till the broken walls be rebuilt.

REBUILDING THE BROKEN WALL NOTES

REBUILDING THE BROKEN WALL NOTES